"I now believe that the use of the Swiss Exercise Ball is a vehicle by which we can be kept in a constant state of awareness while we acquire conducting technique. I have found that if I can maintain a heightened state of awareness while keeping in mind the essentials of Body Mapping while I teach the fundamentals of conducting technique, a new level of "understanding" takes place. When technique is acquired through a heightened state of kinesthetic awareness, it is easy for musical expressivity to be transported and transferred to the ensemble. Those who repeatedly use the Swiss Ball while learning conducting technique can accomplish this almost unknowingly."

James Jordan
Learn Conducting Technique
with the Swiss Exercise Ball

Learn Conducting Technique with the Swiss Exercise Ball

Developing Kinclusive Conducting Awareness

Other publications by James Jordan
available from GIA Publications, Inc.

The Musician's Soul

The Musician's Spirit

The Musician's Walk

Evoking Sound: The Choral Warm-Up
Core Vocal Exercises
with Marilyn Shenenberger

Meditations for the Musician's Soul
by Fr. Bede Camera, O.S.B.,
& James Jordan

Evoking Sound: Fundamentals of Choral Conducting and Rehearsing

Evoking Sound Video
with Heather Buchanan

The Evoking Sound Choral Series

Choral Ensemble Intonation: Method, Ensemble, and Exercises
Text & video
by James Jordan &
Matthew Mehaffey

Ear Training Immersion Exercises for Choirs

Learn Conducting Technique with the Swiss Exercise Ball

DEVELOPING

KINCLUSIVE

CONDUCTING

AWARENESS

JAMES JORDAN

WESTMINSTER CHOIR COLLEGE
OF RIDER UNIVERSITY

GIA Publications, Inc.
Chicago

Learn Conducting Technique with the Swiss Exercise Ball

Developing Kinclusive Conducting Awareness

James Jordan

Companion to Evoking Sound Video Body Mapping Principles and Basic Conducting Technique (GIA, 2002)

G-6478
ISBN: 1-57999-359-1

7404 S. Mason Ave., Chicago, IL 60638
www.giamusic.com

Cover Design/Illustration **Yolanda Durán**
Book Design **Yolanda Durán**
Photography **Eric Kephart, Zonkarts Gallery**
622 South Fifth St., Philadelphia, PA
www.Zonkarts.com

Swiss Ball courtesy of Spri Products

This book is dedicated to three influential conductors, teachers, and friends.

to. . .

Weston Noble

Who has always been aware of life and its connection to music and has taught me and others by example how to make that awareness transfer into beautiful sound.

Barbara Conable

Who, through her teaching gifts, has transformed my thinking, teaching, and music-making as well as that of countless students.

Gail B. Poch

The first conducting teacher of mine who had a passion for conducting pedagogy and made me aware that my body could influence sound.

Table of Contents

Preface

I have many people to thank concerning the material in this book. Since meeting **Barbara Conable** some ten years ago, her teaching at Westminster during Saturday seminars and summer workshops has had a profound influence on the way I rehearse my choir and teach conducting. I hope that her work concerning Body Mapping creates a tidal wave of instructional change within music education and performance. I know that her work contains incredible truth and should become part of the pedagogy of every music teacher and musician. Moreover, she has been a great friend and has shared her knowledge with many. For that, I am deeply grateful. I first saw her use the Swiss Ball with conductors at a Westminster Summer Conducting Symposium.

I would also like to thank my former colleague at Westminster, **Heather Buchanan.** She began as my student, and I am now learning Body Mapping from her. Heather studied with Barbara Conable, and it is her goal to apply Body Mapping to the teaching of conducting. She is a gifted teacher who, like Barbara, is able to articulate Body Mapping principles in a direct and convincing way. I know that her work in this discipline will transform the landscape of how we teach conducting.

I am also grateful to my **conducting students at Westminster** who have endured my experimentation with Swiss Balls and probably hold the record for inflating them. They have provided valuable feedback and insight concerning the use of these Swiss Balls in their classes. In fact, they have demanded that we use them daily. I doubt that I would have pursued the use of the Swiss Balls without their persistence.

Finally, I would like to thank the **North Central ACDA,** the **CBDNA,** and the **Oregon Music Educators Association.** It was because of the enthusiastic response to my clinics during their conventions that this book came to be.

And, as always, thanks go to my publisher, **GIA,** and **Alec Harris,** President. Their unwavering support of new pedagogical directions for music education continues to be an inspiration for my writing. I will always be indebted to them and their wonderful company.

Finally, I am indebted to **Eric Scott Kephart** and **Zonkarts Gallery** (Zonkarts.com) for their photography and ongoing support of my life and work.

The magic of the Swiss Exercise Ball and its value in conducting pedagogy has only just begun. I hope you will find it as valuable a teaching aid as I have.

Introduction

Since I became acquainted with the work of Barbara Conable, my teaching of the conducting art has undergone a constant and steady metamorphosis. Before becoming aware of Barbara's work, I, like so many, used teaching procedures to develop conducting technique in both new students and more advanced students. Most of those techniques involved developing a somewhat "geometric" approach to teaching conducting technique. This includes how big the pattern should be, where the pattern is placed on the body, and so forth.

However, as we all realize, conducting technique is part geometric, part kinesthetic. Because musicians are generally not natural movers, sometimes conducting technique becomes an imitative art. Rarely is conducting technique development associated with sounds and their associated kinesthetic sensations.

Barbara Conable uses the terms awareness and inclusive awareness in her lectures on Body Mapping to describe the heightened kinesthetic state of a musician who moves **with awareness.**

As I ponder the past 20 years of my conducting teaching, I believe I am able to pinpoint the problems that occur in all conductors regardless of their experience or instruction. It seems that we have been teaching conducting, through no fault of our own, with a reliance on a kind of external awareness of how we look rather than how we FEEL, or should FEEL, when we conduct. Many of us, as we continue to conduct, do so in an ever-increasing state of unawareness. The use of videotape has certainly increased our own awareness, but only that kind of awareness, which I like to refer as an outer awareness. I believe that as we as conductors can learn how to move our bodies in a state of kinesthetic awareness that we will move very differently.

History and Philosophy

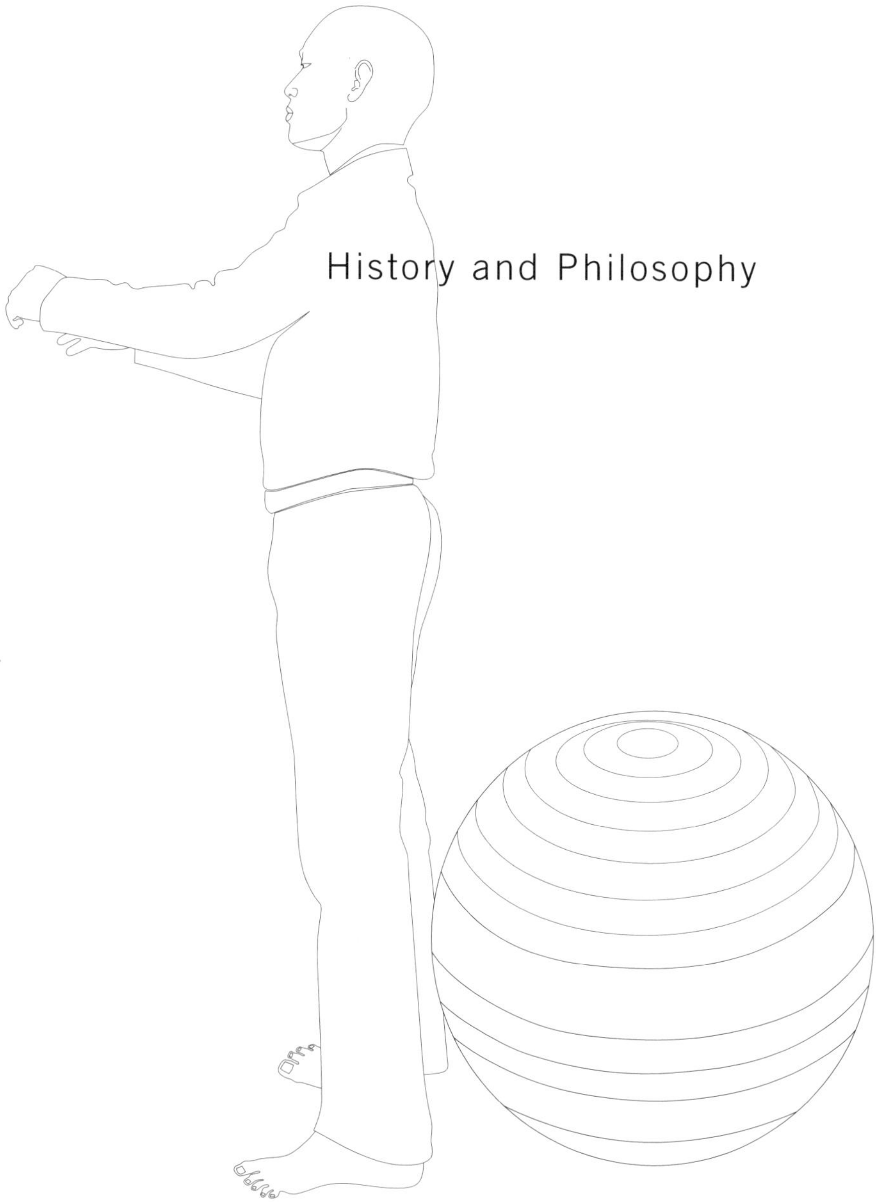

History and Philosophy

A Short History of the Swiss Ball

Large, inflatable vinyl balls were first used in the 1960s by Swiss physical therapists to help children with cerebral palsy facilitate balance and equilibrium reactions. Through awareness gained using the Swiss Ball, therapists found the ball helpful in maintaining coordination and body use. Susanne Klein-Vogelbach, head of the Physiotherapy School in Basel, Switzerland, was one of the first therapists to begin using the Swiss Ball as a therapeutic tool. She incorporated the use of the ball into treatment regimens for neurological and orthopedic patients.

In Europe the use of the ball and what is known as Functional Kinetics are taught in almost every physiotherapy school as basic "reactive exercises." In 1972, Maria Kucera, then a Czech physical therapist, attended one of Klein-Vogelbach's Functional Kinetics courses and was inspired to adopt the use of the Swiss Ball. As a result, she published a book titled *Gymnastic mit dem Hupfball.* This book has been a resource for European physical therapists since 1973.

In the United States, the following therapists have been influential in the development of this instruction: Caroline Creager, Barbara Headley, Dennis Morgan, Beate Carriere, Barbara Hypes, Nancy Good, Joanne Posner-Mayer, and Kathie Hanson.

The Zen of Biking and Conducting

> I feel there's something almost unfair about trying to teach a skill by putting it into words. We learn so much more when we learn through our senses and

> our experience. Maybe there are "information" subjects where verbal instruction works best, but music is something the body is going to have to perform and it's best learned by the body that's going to do the performing. (p. 132)
>
> Barry Green & W. Timothy Gallwey
> *The Inner Game of Music*

Allow me to use a simple analogy to make a point. I do a great deal of biking. Riding a bike requires a constant state of kinesthetic awareness to maintain balance and stay on the bike. When I first took up this hobby, I learned very quickly that in order to avoid physical injury on the bike, I needed to develop a unique sense of awareness when riding. When I first rode, I had many "accidents" along the way; scuffed knees and arms were the norms of the day! I believed that I needed to be on the lookout for potholes and other obstacles that would cause me to lose control of the bike. So, to prevent injury, I focused on avoiding obstacles.

Then I began reading some books on mountain biking. All of the books talk about developing a "general" awareness with no particular focus on any single aspect of the environment. That is, if you focus upon visually sighting trees and rocks, you most certainly will encounter disaster. General awareness, in contrast, instructs you in a kinesthetic way to view everything simultaneously. In order to make the bike part of you, the bike and your physical environment must be perceived constantly as one. In this state of heightened awareness, I find that I can ride a bike through any terrain with no fear of hurting myself.

Any athletic task requires such awareness. The skier has a unique awareness of his whole body as it relates to the skiing surface through the contact with the snow via the ski equipment he or she uses. Baseball players, when they hit a ball, are kinesthetically aware of the relationship of their bodies to the bat and, consequently, to the oncoming ball. Great basketball players have an incredible kinesthetic awareness of themselves as they move through space and around the court before shooting. Kinesthetic awareness is key to all athletic endeavors. That same kinesthetic awareness is essential to the development of conducting technique that evokes a response in musicians within an ensemble.

Unawareness in Musicians

To understand the need for inclusive awareness and how to develop that awareness in conductors, one must first examine what the many reasons for unawareness in musicians are.

First, the study of an instrument and the development of technique on that instrument tends to decrease awareness rather than increase it. In fact, the way we are generally taught any aspect of performance inadvertently develops a type of kinesthetic unawareness that, on a long-term basis, is detrimental to the development of both technique and the musician.

As one learns technique, regardless of the instrument, there is a focus on the fingers, fingering patterns, or specific aspects of the technique that must be developed to "master" the instrument. Over months and years of practice, we tend to develop a type of tunnel-vision focus where we perceive a relatively limited world that involves a relatively limited feedback system in our bodies. We perform etudes with a somewhat limited kinesthetic sense and do rather well with that limited kinesthesia.

It has been my observation that great instrumentalists and singers bring an effortless quality to what they do. One can always hear remarks that "they make it look easy." What makes it looks easy to us? It is the fact that they are in a state of inclusive or total awareness as they perform; that is, they are not "focusing" on any one aspect of their technique, but that performing as an organically whole and kinesthetically alive being allows their "instrument" and THEM to speak.

I was recently involved in a conference at Texas Lutheran University in Texas entitled "The Creative Journey." There was one session that had a profound effect on my thinking about the need for us to teach kinesthetic awareness to our students. Aaron Guidry, a percussionist with *Cirque du Soleil,* gave a presentation on his creative process. Armed with only a set of drumsticks and a drum pad for his presentation, he began by saying, " I really don't know what I do when I create; I just do it." As he was speaking to us, he simultaneously started to improvise on the drum pad! His speech, his body, and his sticks all moved with a rhythmic synchronicity that was astounding. Frankly, I have never witnessed such an incredible display of awareness. While he was speaking, he played some of the most fascinating percussion patterning that I have heard in quite some time. As he concluded this tour de force demonstration, he remarked, "How do I create? I really don't know. I just know that it excites my whole body and that excitement comes through my sticks, and then at the same time I want to communicate what I FEEL to the audience. That's all . . . that's it."

What I had just witnessed was an incredibly kinesthetically gifted musician. Aaron is aware of everything . . . all the time. He is aware of his body, his surroundings, sounds, and his own spirit. His awareness allows him to communicate in the most profound and direct way.

I wondered at the time, "How can we get conductors to a heightened state of awareness where gesture can be transformed from mere physical movement to movement that grows out of inclusive awareness?" I now believe that the use of the

Swiss Exercise Ball is a vehicle through which we can be kept in a constant state of awareness while we acquire conducting technique. I have found that if I can maintain a heightened state of awareness while keeping in mind the essentials of Body Mapping while I teach the fundamentals of conducting technique, a new level of "understanding" takes place. When technique is acquired through a heightened state of kinesthetic awareness, it is easy for musical expressivity to be transported and transferred to the ensemble. Those who repeatedly use the Swiss Ball while learning conducting technique can accomplish this almost unknowingly.

The Dilemma of an Unaware World

This issue of unawareness is such a serious problem in the training of musicians because the world we live in breeds unawareness. In this increasingly complex world, in order to survive on a day-to-day basis we develop devices that "keep us safe." Through our day-to-day routines in this humanly damaging world, we erect defenses to protect ourselves. Aside from the spiritual defenses necessary to survive, I believe that we have become increasingly unaware from a kinesthetic perspective. We are numb to the world and numb to our bodies because we associate that detachment with safety. The irony lies in the fact that we increase our unawareness at an exponential rate by establishing unawareness as the normal bodily feeling. We are out of touch with the feeling of our bodies because the world has done this to us. Increased reliance on computers as a means of communication and knowledge acquisition has not helped the cause of kinesthetic awareness. While it seems to be a simple device, the Swiss Exercise Ball both compels and empowers our awareness. While we are seated on that ball, our kinesthetic awareness is heightened and maintained as long as we remain on the ball, hence its value in the teaching of conducting.

Building Awareness Through the Swiss Ball

I believe that one of the major pedagogical missteps in conducting pedagogy and in music instruction in general is that there is undue emphasis upon "focus" rather than building awareness in musicians and, in this case, conductors. We have always been taught that we need to "focus" on aspects of our musicianship. Focus (on hands, technique, pitch, rhythm, etc.) seems to have been a mantra of instruction. Such an emphasis on "focus" creates the opposite effect over a long period of time. In our attempt to "focus" we, in essence, are condoning an increasing state of unawareness in us and in the musicians we teach. We should abolish the word "focus" from our teaching language and substitute the word "awareness."

Awareness in musicians should at all times be multi-faceted and all-inclusive. In addition to being aware of musical elements that come through hearing, we need to have a highly developed kinesthetic sense. We need to be intimately aware of our bodies at all times during the music-making process. If we expect our ensembles to play with an "alive" and inspirited sound, then we must conduct in an aware and enlivened state. We need to be aware of our entire body ALL the time. Incessant kinesthetic feedback from our bodies should be the norm for music making.

This type of awareness is difficult to describe, but it is even more difficult to teach and more difficult still to learn! I believe the use of the Swiss Ball immediately moves conducting pedagogy to the realm of teaching awareness through constant kinesthetic feedback.

Staying in Touch with Energy Flow: Swiss Ball Feedback for Life

> Well, and what is freedom? First of all, freedom seems to mean the absence of external restraint, the freedom to play. When we are free from external tyrannies, we seek freedom from our inner limitations. We find that in order to play we must be nimble and flexible and imaginative, we must be able to have fun, we must feel enjoyment, and sometimes long imprisonment has made us numb and sluggish. And then we find out that there are, paradoxically, disciplines which create in us capacities which allow us to seek our freedom. We learn how to rid ourselves of boredom, of stiffness, our repressed anger, and our anxiety. We become brighter, more energy flows through us, our limbs rise, and our spirit comes alive in our tissues. (p. 22)
>
> Mary Caroline Richards
> *Centering in Pottery, Poetry, and the Person*

The use of the Swiss Ball seems to remedy another problem for conductors. Over a period of time, one may become aware that energy flow to the ensemble has been blocked because of alignment issues. Unless one is really "aurally tuned" and sensitive to hearing subtle changes of sound in the ensemble, poor usage can creep into one's conducting technique almost without notice.

If one learns conducting technique on the Swiss Ball, one will learn that the ball responds with small bounces or recoils when energy is being released from one's body into the ball. This continual kinesthetic feedback maintains one's state of awareness. Many people think that if they learn or relearn conducting technique on the ball, once learned, the changes are permanent. **They are not.** One must continually return to the Swiss Ball for "kinesthetic" tune-ups! Stated in another way, you must use the Swiss Ball for the rest of your conducting career! To do so will ensure good usage and expressive technique, and, more important, encourage free and resonant sound from your ensemble.

Body Mapping: Supplemental Resources for Use with This Text

> Music Education belongs on a somatic foundation because musicians move for a living, like dancers and athletes, except that musicians' movement is even more refined, precise and rapid (p. 4)
>
> The Body Map is one's self-representation in one's own brain. If the Body Map is accurate, movement is good. If the Body Map is inaccurate or inadequate, movement is inefficient and injury producing. In Body Mapping, one learns to gain access to one's own Body Map through self-observation and self-inquiry. One carefully examines what one believes to be true about his or her own body by comparing it to accurate information provided by kinesthetic experience, mirrors, books, pictures, and teachers. One thereby learns to recognize the source of inefficient or harmful movement and how to replace it with movement that is efficient, elegant, direct and powerful based on the truth about one's structure, function and size (p. 5)
>
> Barbara Conable
> *What Every Musician Needs to Know About the Body:The Practical Application of Body Mapping & the Alexander Technique to Making Music*

This book will not review *Body Mapping Principles,* which are clearly and beautifully discussed in two publications. The Swiss Exercise Ball exercises cannot be used without using Body Mapping principles as put forward in the *Evoking Sound Video: Body Mapping Principles and Basic Conducting Technique* by Heather Buchanan and me (GIA, 2002). The way we "input" conducting technique needs to change. When teaching conducting technique, we MUST teach our students how our bodies actually move and not rely on their fantasies of how they move. Further, we must teach conductors to be more kinesthetically aware as they conduct.

All teachers and students of conducting must realize that very few of us have accurate Body Maps of ourselves. That is, we have little or no clue how our body actually "works." Body Mapping has taught me that self-awareness cannot be assumed. Care and time taken in conducting classes to teach three major aspects necessary to developing conducting technique (1) *the core of the body,* (2) *the breath process,* and (3) *the correct structure of the arm and hand,* will reap benefits beyond your imagination. The above-mentioned video is a necessary companion to the exercises and approach presented in this book.

My second and strong recommendation is that every student of conducting have read and have access to another important work on Body Mapping: *What Every Musician Needs to Know About the Body: The Practical Application of Body Mapping and the Alexander Technique to Making Music* by Barbara Conable, with illustrations by Benjamin Conable (Portland, Oregon: Andover Press, 2000). Students using this text must become familiar with the material presented in the chapters The Head and Neck, The Spine, The Torso, The Legs, The Arms, and The Hands. The illustrations in that book are an important part of the Body Mapping process.

Importance of Inside Development

Another word of caution: In **tandem** with learning conducting technique using Body Mapping principles taught via the Swiss Exercise Ball, one must always keep in mind the principles necessary for the development of the "insides" of the musician. The inside of the musician is extensively developed in three publications. The concept and overall philosophy of "inside" development is put forward in the conducting text *Evoking Sound* (GIA, 1996). The concepts outlined in the early chapters of that book are further discussed in *The Musician's Soul* (GIA, 2000) and *The Musician's Spirit* (GIA, 2003). Both of these books need to be used at the same time that conducting technique is being learned. Conducting technique is at once a development of an awareness that includes BOTH a constant awareness of the body and a simultaneous awareness of one's spirit. I believe that the term INCLUSIVE AWARENESS for conductors connotes a simultaneous awareness of both the kinesthetic and the spiritual that can be then transmitted through sound. Consider the following paradigm for the development of a total conductor:

Communicative Expressive Gesture Formula

Body Mapping + Inside Spiritual Actualization

= Kinesthetic Awareness^2

To interpret my mathematical analogy above, the effectiveness of any gesture, no matter how well taught, is always mitigated by the state (or lack thereof) of inclusive kinesthetic awareness of the conductor at any one moment in time. That inclusive awareness must always be present for a meaningful gesture to be realized that will, in turn, profoundly affect musical performance.

Understanding the Core of the Body

> An act of the self, that's what one must make. An act of the self, from me to you. From center to center. We must mean what we say, from our innermost heart to the outermost galaxy. Otherwise we are lost and dizzy in a maze of reflections. We carry light within us. There is no need merely to reflect. Others carry light within them. These lights must wake each other. My face is real. Yours is. Let us find our way to our initiative. (p. 18)
>
> Mary Caroline Richards
> *Centering in Pottery, Poetry, and the Person*

Considering the content included on the *Evoking Sound* video, one should not underestimate the importance of the constant awareness of the core of the body in the process of developing and rehabilitating conducting technique. There is a striking commonality among ALL conducting students that I have taught over the years. All of them share one major "technical" problem in their conducting. I also have found that almost all conducting technique problems have their genesis or root at the same place. These conductors are unaware, almost all the time, of the CORE of their body. Body Mapping teaches us that the body is organized like an apple around a core. While that is a powerful analogy in and of itself, one can understand the cognitive description of the body without ever **feeling** the core of the body. Or rather, being in a state of continual awareness of the core of the body while one is conducting and making music. Awareness of the core of the body is, I feel, the keystone to the development of meaningful and expressive conducting technique. That is, one must be in a state of **constant** kinesthetic awareness of WHERE that core of the body is perceived. Prior to this, while I believed that "alignment" was a contributory factor to the development of expressive technique, I never realized that it came down to the kinesthetic awareness of that core of the body. A constant awareness of the pelvis and the central location of the four lumbar vertebrae are pivotal to conductor awareness and expressivity. Only through vigilant use of the Swiss Exercise Ball can this be accomplished and made a natural part of one's awareness.

Developing Greater Kinesthetic Awareness with the Swiss Ball

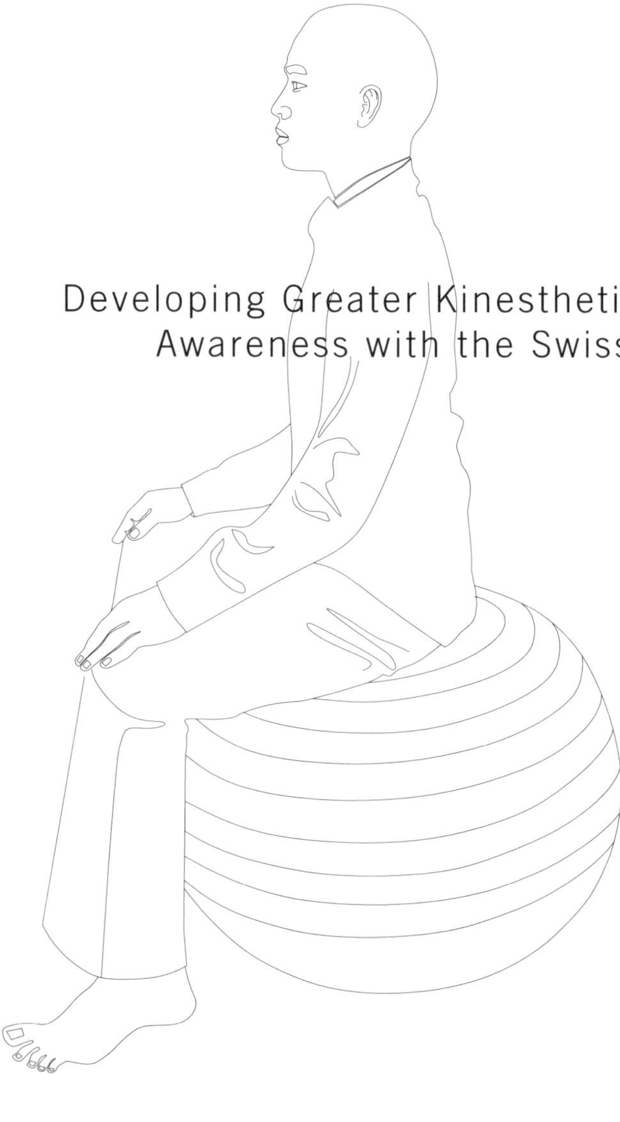

Developing Greater Kinesthetic Awareness with the Swiss Ball

The Power of the Swiss Exercise Ball: Why It Works

First, consider the following definitions of the words **kinesthesia** and **balance.** Balance is a word that may be somewhat familiar, while kinesthesia may not be so familiar. Pay particular attention to those definitions in boldface.

kin·es-the-sia or kin-es-the-sis *(noun)*

The perception or sensing of the motion, weight, or position of the body as muscles, tendons, and joints move. Also called muscle sense.

bal·ance

(noun)

1. a state in which a body or object remains reasonably steady in a particular position while resting on a base that is narrow or small relative to its other dimensions.
2. **a state in which two opposing forces or factors are of equal strength or importance so that they effectively cancel each other out and stability is maintained.**
3. **a state in which various elements form a satisfying and harmonious whole and nothing is out of proportion or unduly emphasized at the expense of the rest.**
4. a state of emotional and mental stability in which somebody is calm and able to make rational decisions and judgments.
5. a simple mechanical device for weighing objects or samples, often consisting of a pivoted horizontal beam with a pan suspended from each end.

(balance continued)

6. something that offsets or counters the weight or influence of another element.

(verb)

1. (vti) to achieve or maintain, or cause somebody or something to achieve or maintain a position of steadiness while resting on a narrow base.
2. (vti) to place an object in a position where it is or seems to be in imminent danger of falling over or of falling off something (often passive).
3. (vt) to assess and compare the relative importance of different factors or alternatives before making a choice or decision.
4. (vt) to weigh something in a balance or by an action or method that resembles the working of a balance.
5. (vti) to be equal to something in force, weight, or importance, or cancel it out.
6. **(vt) to arrange the different elements of something so that they form a harmonious and well-proportioned whole.**

Having considered the above definitions, now try to arrive at a definition of awareness of the core of the body. To be kinesthetically aware, one must be kept in a constant state of kinesthetic awareness! Words and explanations are woefully inadequate to elect such a heightened state of awareness. Resorting to verbal explanations and reminders are, to put it bluntly, totally ineffective. The concept of the Swiss Exercise Ball is stupendously simple. The balls were first developed for use in the health spas of Switzerland to help persons with cerebral palsy regain awareness lost because of the disease. The balls were designed as a therapeutic aid to help persons regain lost awareness and sensations of physical balance, a remarkable invention, to be sure.

Just as the Swiss Exercise Balls were designed to rejuvenate sensations of balance and a heightened or newfound sense of awareness, they can perform the same function in conducting pedagogy! Simply sitting and maintaining your "balance" on the ball forces you into many awarenesses about the core of your body. In fact, you not only become aware of the core of your body, but you become aware of your entire body, from a **kinesthetic** perspective. The irony about being kinesthetically aware is that when you are in your most heightened state of awareness about your core, you feel as if no work is being done to maintain your balance on the ball! You are guaranteed to be aware of the core of your body and in balance when you feel as if no work were being done to keep your body on the ball. So, the seemingly simple act of sitting on one of these balls ensures that you will be brought into a heightened level of awareness. If you are not aware of the core of your body, you WILL fall off the ball. It is that simple!

Caution: Be sure to select a ball that is appropriate to your height. You should be offered a full selection of balls (at least three sizes) that coincide with your height!

Somatic Awareness vs. Kinclusive Awareness

so·mat-ic *(adjective)*

1. relating to or affecting the body, especially the body as considered to be separate from the mind.
2. relating to the outer walls of the body, not the inner organs.
3. relating to a somatic cell.

The Swiss Ball builds what is called **somatic awareness.** Somatics is the study of Body Mapping and the relationship of that mapping to actual body function. If a Body Map is corrected, the use of that portion of the body that was "remapped" is corrected forever. Likewise, if a body is remapped AND that new usage is acquired while on a Swiss Ball, a new awareness is developed, an awareness of both Body Mapping and the feeling of that new usage, somatic awareness. For instructional clarity, I have coined the term **kinclusive awareness.** The Swiss Ball marries kinesthetic awareness and the newly acquired sense of inclusive awareness (awareness of the entire body). Because these two new awarenesses are perceived while moving and hearing music, I wanted a term that would label the concurrent perceptions of the Body Map and the Core of the Body combined with kinesthesia and its concurrent relationship to sound, hence the term ***kinclusive awareness.*** **Kinclusive awareness is multidimensional.**

The Need for Both Kinesthetic and Visual Feedback

Another value of the Swiss Exercise Ball is that it provides a radically different system of feedback that is both immediate and powerful for the conducting student. Heretofore, all of the feedback that conductors received about their conducting related to a viewing of a videotape of their conducting. While such tapes can provide valuable visual feedback, it is the type of feedback that is most inefficient for conductors. Viewing of videotapes provides an external manifestation of conducting technique. Hence, all corrections of that technique will most likely be external and will not be brought into the realm of kinesthetic awareness. Two strategies are suggested to remedy this serious problem.

Two Modes of Evaluating Videotape

We need to change the way information is gathered from videotape. Students should view videotapes in **each** of two modes. First, play the tape with the sound off. When seen in this way, students are forced to evaluate the efficiency and correctness of the movement with respect to Body Mapping principles. When sound is present, the viewer may assume that his or her movement is good if the sound is acceptable. In fact, it may not be so good! Viewing a tape with the sound off ensures that movement alone will be evaluated.

Second, watch the tape again with the sound off, but this time view the tape in fast forward. This technique quickly locates idiosyncratic movements of which a person may be unaware.

Correcting Conducting Technique

Once you have ascertained the corrections that need to be made via your videotape evaluation, process the correction while sitting on a Swiss Exercise Ball. By doing this, you will learn to correct your technique kinesthetically, rather than cognitively. Movement will be then internalized, rather than relying on the older pedagogy of correcting movement externally.

Conducting Video Evaluation Form

To assist students with this evaluative process, use the following form to ensure that they evaluate their conducting gesture correctly with respect to Body Mapping principles as discussed on the Evoking Sound video. A new form should be completed each time one videotapes!

Conducting Critique/Self-Analysis

Name

Work

Date

Body Mapping Analysis ***(Volume Off)***

Six points of balance?

Correct use of arm?

Employment of all joints?

Correct usage of ulnar movement?

Is humero-scapular movement and freedom present?

Is there an awareness of the body present?

Use of Ictus ***(Volume On)***

Is there a clear rhythmic impulse?

Is the ictus released?

Is the conductor able to impel the musical line?

Stereotypical Movements ***(Volume Off and Fast Forward)***

What problematic stereotypical movements are present?

Perceived **Openness** and **Listening** and **Reacting**

Is the anticipatory gesture "open?"

Are you listening?

Are you reacting to the sound?

Is there a clear atmosphere of care and love as music is being made?

Change of Focus or **Shift of Attention**

Are you tracking musical lines?

Are you in a constant state of awareness?

New Conducting Technique Through Kinesthetic Awareness

The use of the Swiss Exercise Ball can avoid many, if not most, of the problems encountered when learning conducting technique from the beginning. It must be repeated, however, that before the Swiss Ball is employed, the user MUST have viewed the Evoking Sound video. Not having a thorough background in Body Mapping before using the Swiss Ball may create many technical problems. It is important that one thoroughly understand (1) the core of the body and (2) have the six points of balance clearly mapped in one's mind, especially points 1 and 4. View the diagram on page 30 after watching the video. It should reinforce knowledge about the core of the body and the mapping of the six points of balance. Note the vertical dotted line that drops through the center of the diagram. This is the "core" around which the entire body is organized. It then needs to be perceived as a central core just as an apple is organized around its core.

One must also be familiar with the correct mapping of the arm. The following points must be thoroughly understood before any development of technique on the ball can occur. The points that MUST be familiar are as follows:

- The location of axis for each arm
- Number and location of the joints in each arm
- Accurate Body Map of wrist
- The location of the scapula

Be clear about the three areas of rotation in the arm: (1) ulnar rotation (as demonstrated with "dots" on the video), (2) the upper arm, and (3) humero-scapular rotation as also explained on the video.

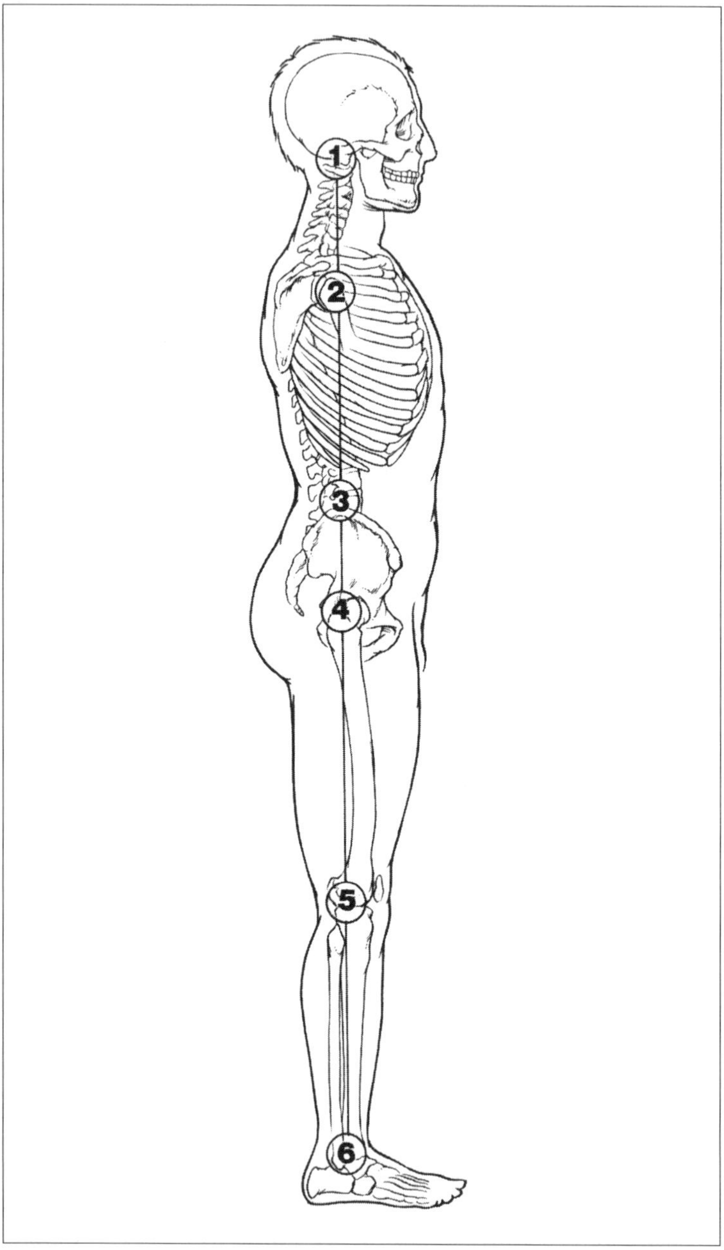

Figure 1: The six points of balance and the core of the body

Staying on Your Core

> To formulate Alexander's discoveries as Laws of Human Movement, laws in the Scientific sense, universal and invariable. I believe there are two.
>
> 1. Habituated tensing of the muscles of the neck results in a predictable and inevitable tensing of the whole body. Release out of the tensing of the whole must begin with release of the muscles of the neck.
>
> 2. In movement, when it's free, the head leads and the body follows. More particularly, the head leads and the spine follows in sequence. (p. 3)
>
> But here's the rub. The pattern of tensing Alexander called downward pull interferes or opposes or counters the involuntary patterns that support us. Typically, those involuntary reflex patterns lengthen us, especially when they involve the spine. Downward pull shortens us. (p. 8–9)
>
> The word waist dominates our mapping and therefore our moving. I say the word, and not the thing, because a waist is a fiction, a kinesthetic fantasy. Something arbitrary, and nothing anatomical, is named in the word waist . . .. The central organizing feature in the body is not horizontal, but vertical. It is the spine.
>
> To add insult to injury, we call our waist our middle. It is not. Our middle is the pelvic floor. We are divided in half at the hip joint. (p. 44)
>
> Barbara Conable and William Conable
> *How to Learn the Alexander Technique: A Manual for Students*

By using the Swiss Ball, the integrity of the core of the body is kept intact. That is, the "lengthening" relationship between points 4 and 1 of the core of the body is maintained through the awareness created simply from sitting on the Swiss Ball. One simply cannot sit on the ball and not be immediately aware of one's core. Further, I have found that unawareness of the core is one of the most serious hindrances toward the development of an expressive, communicative conducting technique.

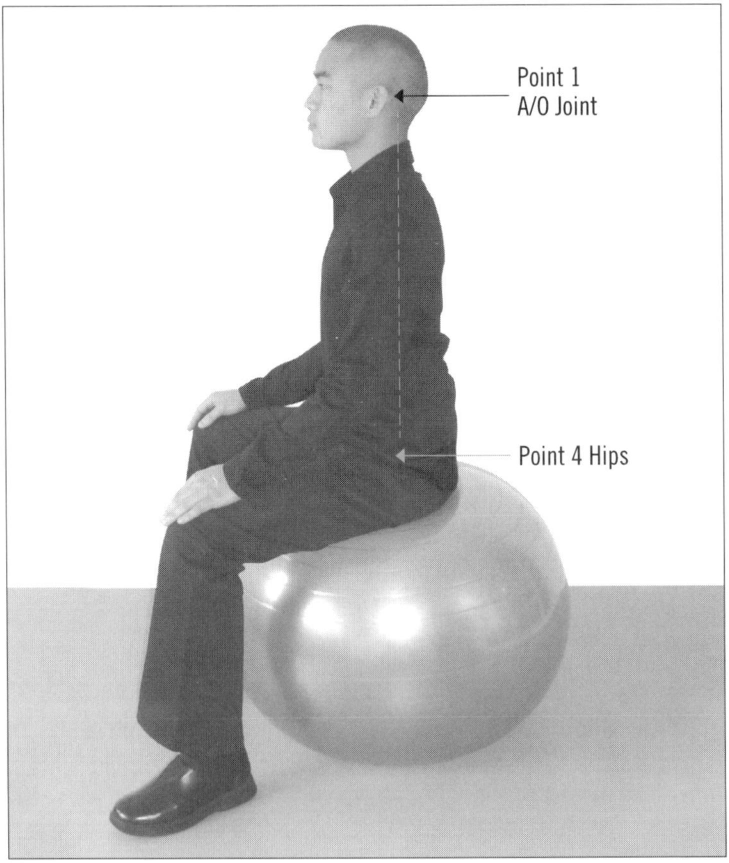

Figure 2: Points 4 (hips and lower lumbar vertebrae) and 1 (the A/O joint) in correct relationship on the Swiss Ball (side view)

The A/O Joint: "Control" Center for Conductors

Of all the points of balance and all the joints that must be correctly mapped for free and unencumbered motion to be realized, no joint carries as much influence upon the sound of the ensemble as the A/O joint. This joint is referred to as the A/O joint because the atlas (the top vertebrae) meets the occipital (the base of the skull), hence the abbreviations A/O. This joint at the top of the spine has two condiles or cups as part of its structure. The entire weight of the head balances on that "joint." Nerve pathways for the body and auditory nerves also pass through the A/O joint. When the body is improperly aligned, the head drags in a downward and forward direction, placing pressure on this joint. Alexander Technique refers to this as the downward/forward pull. That downward/forward pull places pressure upon the A/O joint and the nerve bundle that passes through that joint. The result for the conductor is that hearing and overall kinesthetic sensitivity is reduced! While the effect on the conductor is profound, the effects upon the ensemble are even more far reaching. Any pressure from the conductor's downward pull will negatively affect the sound of the ensemble. The color of the sound will dull, and pitch problems will appear.

Mapping of the A/O joint is difficult because it resides in the interior central core of the skull. The illustrations below will help correct your map of the A/O joint. If you look at the following front view of the skull, you will notice that the skull is in its proper frontal alignment.

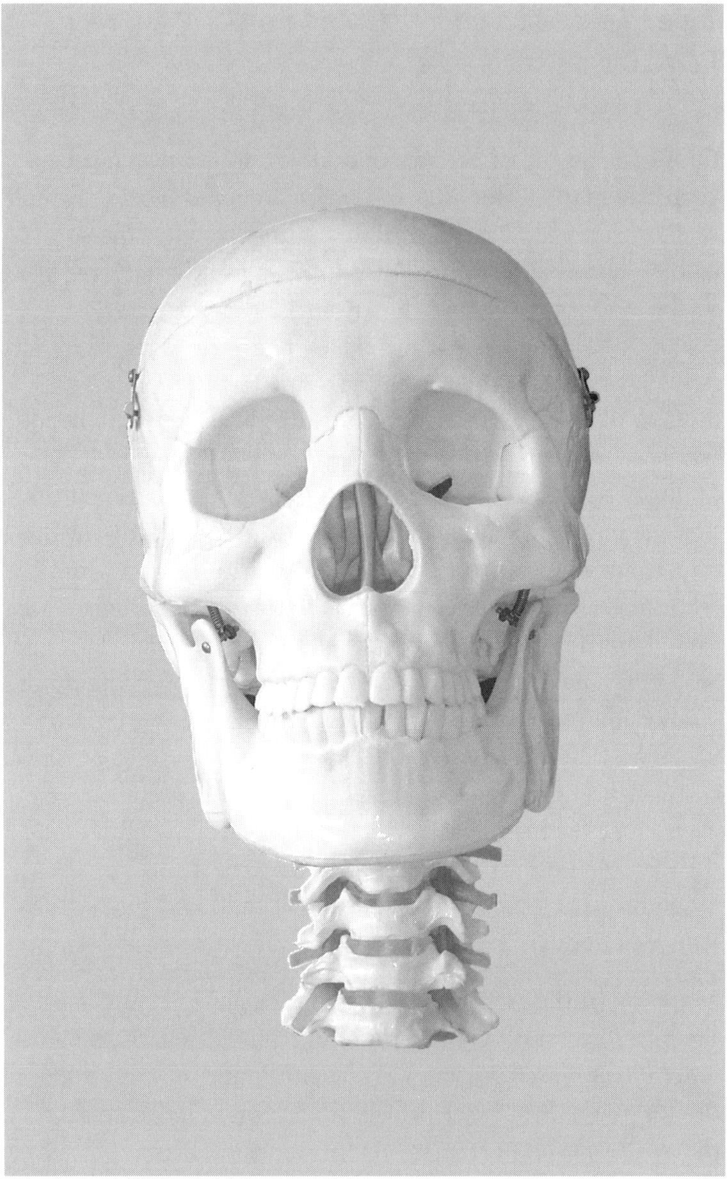

Figure 3: Front view of skull. The A/O joint is within the skull, between the ears, and directly behind the nose in the center of the skull.

Examining the skull and the A/O joint from a side perspective makes it look like the skull is out of line and leaning slightly backward. This is the correct alignment of the A/O joint! Many persons in a correctly aligned state claim that they feel as though they are falling slightly backward. Because they have habitualized a downward/forward pull, the correct alignment will feel as though they are falling backward. The following figure illustrates this point.

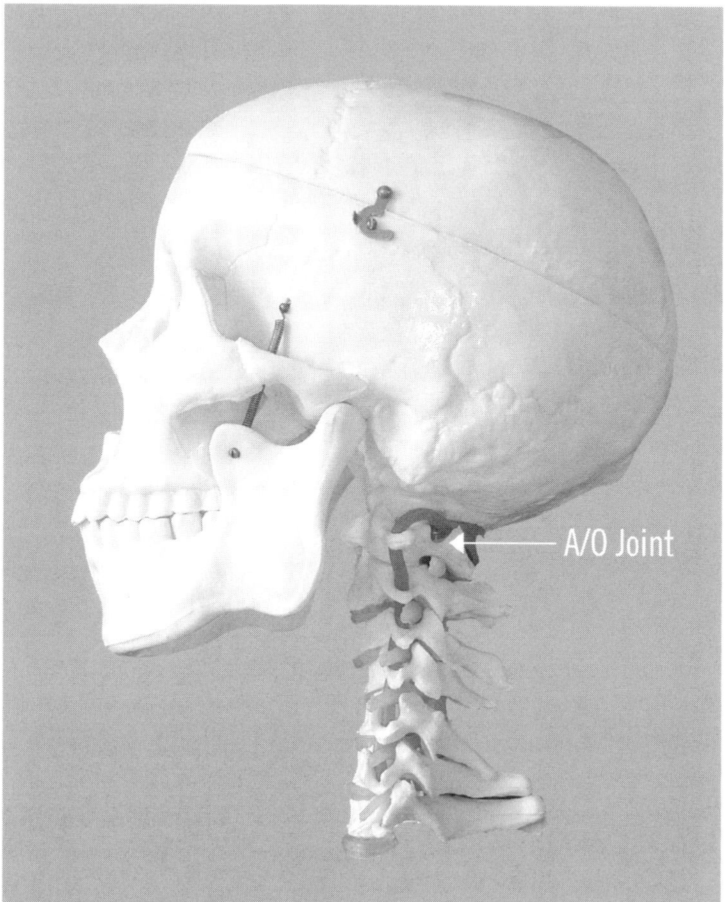

Figure 4: Side view of skull, correctly aligned A/O joint

The Spiritual Core

> I believe in man's unconscious, the deep spring from which comes his power to communicate and to love. For me, all art is a combination of these powers; art is nothing to me if it does not make contact between the creator and the perceiver on an unconscious level. Let us say that love is the way we have of communicating personally in the deepest way. What art can do is to extend this communication, magnify it, and carry it to vastly greater numbers of people. In this it needs a warm core, a hidden heating element. Without that core, art is only an exercise in techniques, a calling of attention to the artist, or a vain display. I believe in art for the warmth and love it carries within it, even if it be the lightest entertainment, or the bitterest satire, or the most shattering tragedy. For if art is cold it cannot communicate anything to anybody. (pp. 141–142)
>
> Leonard Bernstein
> *Findings*

This particular element is not dealt with on the *Evoking Sound* video and is a relatively recent development in my thinking. The existence and perception of a "core" is extremely important to conductors for establishing a human connection to the ensemble. When you encounter another person for the first time, you are immediately aware of that person and that person's "energy." That energy radiates from a central midline of the body that extends from the core of the body within the pelvis upward in a vertical "column" to the face. This life-energy core transmits non-verbal **human** information about that person as long as you are in spatial contact with him or her. When a musician develops conducting technique, each of the hands, especially the dominant hand, can enter into the core at times to execute patterns. However, at no time, or rather very few times, should that core be blocked or obstructed by the hands. When one constantly conducts obstructing the core, he or she limits or stops the transfer of his or her own human energy and qualities to the ensemble. The lack of this "core" energy that may be hidden behind the gesture will profoundly impact the sound of the ensemble, whether instrumental or vocal.

Energy Projection of the Core to the Ensemble

There are many reasons why someone might block their core. For some, it is a simple technical misunderstanding. Conducting technique needs to develop on each separate and distinct axis, which is on each side of the body as demonstrated on the *Evoking Sound video*. When developing conducting technique it is important to stay away from the midline of the body. Crossing the midline of the body "confuses" the neurological pathways that control free and effortless movement. Excessive work **on** or **crossing** over the midline confuses and slows neurological energy throughout the nerve pathways. Many times the result is loss of pattern, which most often culminates in a kinesthetic imbalance. That is, there is a peculiar absence of kinesthetic awareness when one works on the midline. Stated in another way, inclusive awareness becomes somewhat hampered by working consistently in the core. That is not to say that one cannot pass through the core. Passing through is a natural thing to do. Keeping one's technique in the core, however, has a detrimental effect on both the development of conducting technique and the communication of human qualities to the ensemble.

There is another reason why a conductor may "veer" into the core, sometimes unaware that he or she is doing so. This is an issue of vulnerability or lack thereof. If you have not made peace with your own understanding of vulnerability, and if you are not in a vulnerable state when you learn conducting technique, you may subconsciously "hide" from the ensemble by placing your hands over your core. That human core cannot be perceived by the ensemble. Conductors also tend to do this when they are fearful of some musical issue within the ensemble. If the concept of vulnerability is new to you, it is suggested that you read the chapter on vulnerability in *The Musician's Soul* (GIA, 2000).

> Transparency is vulnerability. It is the capacity to be open within ourselves in order that the music can flow through us—that we can be an open conduit, a free vessel. If we are not vulnerable as conductors, if we don't have the freedom to allow ourselves to be as we are, we can't take experiences offered to us by our singers and incorporate them with our own. Music does not flow through an impeded conduit. As Leonard Bernstein once said, "If the heart isn't free, the baton isn't free." How true. Thus we must work to increase the depth of our feeling function. This will lead to openness, the ability to share our inner person more freely. As we reach a deeper understanding of ourselves, we will gain deeper insights into the spirit of the music.
>
> Vulnerability can be threatening. It is not easy to be open—to share our deepest feelings. And we have

> a shadow side to our lives that tries to block our transparency/vulnerability. We therefore make friends with our shadow side. The accomplishment of this is one of the great adventures of life! A strong shadow results in negative thinking while a friendly shadow results in positive thinking. How can the wonderful beauty of music come forward if our thinking is predominantly negative! (p. 12)
>
> Weston Noble in an interview with Dennis Shrock
> *The Choral Journal*

The Dynamic Core: The Second Dimension

The spiritual core can be perceived as a **vertical** space that remains relatively unencumbered so that spiritual qualities transfer to those who can see it. There is another core that is equally important. Picture the anticipatory position for conducting that reflects a human embrace. That embrace could surround an imaginary cylinder that has both height and depth. The height dimension is the dimension that the spiritual core could occupy. The circumference and depth of the cylinder I refer to as the Dynamic Core. You could also perceive a large egg shape that occupies the space between the arms. That egg-shaped Dynamic Core has a depth that must be maintained at all times. For more intimate moments, the depth of the cylinder and the overall size of the egg may decrease. For larger sound, the depth and size would increase. In both cases, working around that core will elicit a rounder response from the ensemble.

The position of the hands has much to do with the perception of that core. If the hands are too close or too far away, energy is lost to the ensemble. A happy and comfortable medium must be established.

I have found an incredible benefit to the use of the Swiss Ball in my teaching. I have always believed that the curve and arch-like geometry is the stuff of great music. When students learn conducting technique while sitting on the Swiss Ball, it is difficult for them to use any gesture that does not reflect the curve of the ball. I have found the subconscious influence of the Swiss Ball to be both powerful and profound. That influence in conducting practice becomes a living reminder of the incredible dynamic of both the circle and the sphere.

Michael Graves, the great American architect and designer, has remarked that he believes the egg to be the greatest design shape that has ever existed. He makes the egg part of every design he creates that has contact with a human hand. The egg is perfect in symmetry. If one imagines the shape of an egg that can change size according to the musical intent that occupies the space within the arms, both the Spiritual Core (vertical aspect) and the Dynamic Core (depth), which influences the color of the sound, will both always be present in one's gesture as a valuable communicative tool.

Selecting a Swiss Exercise Ball of the Correct Size

It is important for you to select a Swiss Exercise Ball that is appropriate for your height. A ball that is too small will create as many problems with alignment as it solves. Likewise, a ball that is too large will create serious alignment problems. Most companies that market such Swiss Exercise Balls have them in the following standardized sizes. Select the ball appropriate to your height. If your height is at the upper end of the criteria, I would probably suggest the next largest size. The Swiss Balls distributed by GIA are sold in the sizes below and come with a hand pump for inflation. Test for the correctness of the ball size by draping yourself

Formula

45 cm	Under 5'
55 cm	5' to 5' 8"
65 cm	5' 9" to 6' 3"
75 cm	6' 3"

over the ball. The size of the ball should equal the distance between your shoulder and wrist. Another way to test is to sit on the ball. Your hips and the knees should form a 90-degree angle when seated.

Caution! Before using these Swiss Balls, make certain that the ball is fully inflated. The surface of the ball should be quite firm to the touch. Under-inflated Swiss Balls will not accomplish the alignment objectives that make their use such a great aid to developing conducting technique. A fully inflated Swiss Ball is recommended because it has less contact area with the floor, moves quickly, and therefore challenges balance reactions more than an under-inflated ball. *An under-inflated Swiss Ball has greater floor contact area, moves more slowly, and therefore requires less energy to balance.*

Constructive Rest

Before beginning any conducting session or rehearsal, it advantageous to start with a short period of constructive rest on the Swiss Exercise Ball. Kneel with the ball in front of you. Drape your body over the ball. Your abdomen should contact the ball. The arms should drape in a relaxed fashion around the ball. All should be quiet, and you should take this time to be silent and breathe. (Listen to your breath, and use the time to quiet your body.) By draping yourself in this way, you allow your spine to lengthen and lose the tensions of the day that cause your spine to assume a position without an upward release. The more time that you can spend in constructive rest, the more you will realign your body in an appropriate way to develop conducting technique. Also, as one has technique development sessions on the ball, it is helpful to divert those sessions to intermittent periods of constructive rest to rejuvenate alignment and reinforce correct alignment sensations.

Figure 5: Constructive rest position on the Swiss Ball

Use of the Swiss Ball to Experience "Letting Go"

One of the most difficult problems for both beginning and experienced conductors is being able to "let go" of their bodies and gestures in such a way that allows for a freedom in the sound and sound production of the ensemble. Many times this results from a combination of muscular tension and improper alignment. The use of the Swiss Ball makes significant progress toward either partial elimination or total elimination of this problem. In order to sit on the Swiss Ball, one must reorganize the core of the body immediately or risk falling off the ball. Also, in order to stay on the ball you must stay in a state of overall body awareness. Many times the problems with conductors are due to the fact that they are not constantly monitoring their bodies. Severe alignment problems begin to unknowingly manifest themselves. Left uncorrected, an faulty kinesthetic sense of body alignment is then established, which then severely compromises conducting technique. Natural musical impulses are then greatly reduced or stopped because they cannot travel freely and unencumbered through the neural pathways to the ensemble. Using the Swiss Ball puts you in constant touch with your body. Self-monitoring of alignment is continuous. Over time, severe alignment issues disappear.

Beginning Your Work on the Swiss Exercise Ball

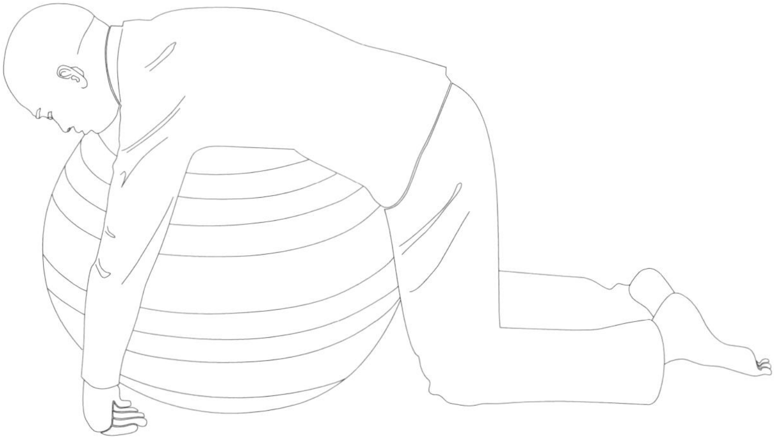

Beginning Your Work on the Swiss Exercise Ball

> Alexander first of all discovered that the relationship of his head and neck had immediate consequences for the condition of his larynx and breathing mechanism and then that the Use of his head and neck was the prime factor in coordinating the Use of the rest of his organism. He functioned best when his stature lengthened, and this came about when he allowed a Use of his head that he described as "forward and up" in relation to his neck and torso. The reader will recall that when Alexander first tried to "put" his head forward and up he found that he could not do so. Eventually, he realized that to achieve his goal he should not "do" or "put" anything, but rather apply a process of non-interfering (inhibition) and conscious reasoned intention (direction). (p. 42)
>
> Michael Gelb
> *Body Learning: An Introduction to the Alexander Technique*

Proper approach to sitting on the Swiss Ball is central to efficient conducting technique development. If you sit on the ball correctly, you automatically organize yourself around the central core of the body. Some may have difficulty initially sitting on the ball because they are not organized around their core. Also, there is a difference between perching oneself on the ball and sitting on the ball. Many persons will perch themselves on the ball, almost like sitting on the edge of a stool, using the legs as both weight bearing and balancing. This position produces undue leg tension and does not achieve organization around the core. To achieve a "perch" one must come "off center" and lean slightly forward to transfer one's weight to the legs.

The proper way to sit on the Swiss Ball is to place your buttocks clearly on the top center of the ball. Legs should contact the floor comfortably and be at least the width of the pelvis apart. When you are "seated" on the ball correctly, you will feel as if no work is being done, and you should also be able to imagine a lengthening between points 4 and 1 from the body diagram above. Aligning to begin conducting work feels effortless and not "held" in place by muscles in any part of the body.

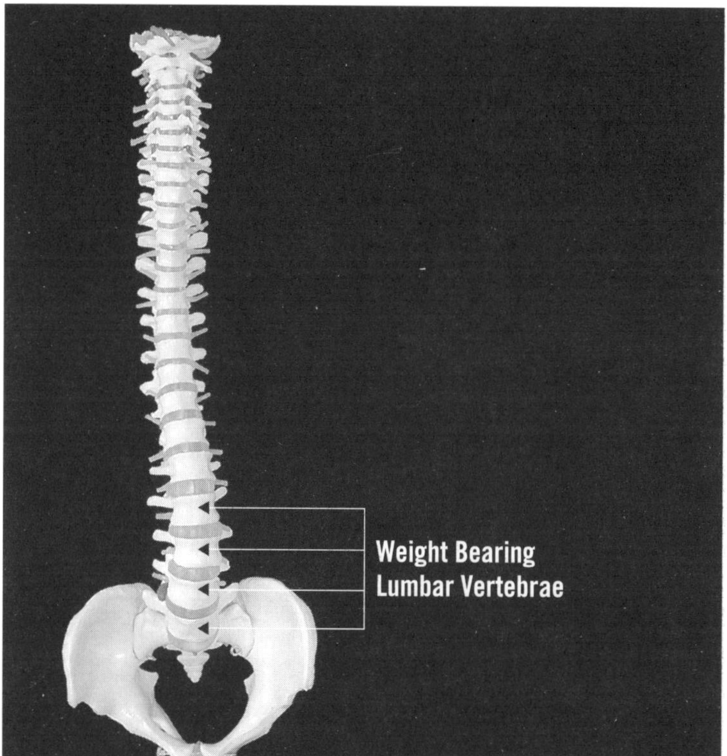

Figure 6: Spinal column (front view) from A/O joint to pelvis with weight-bearing lumbar vertebrae identified

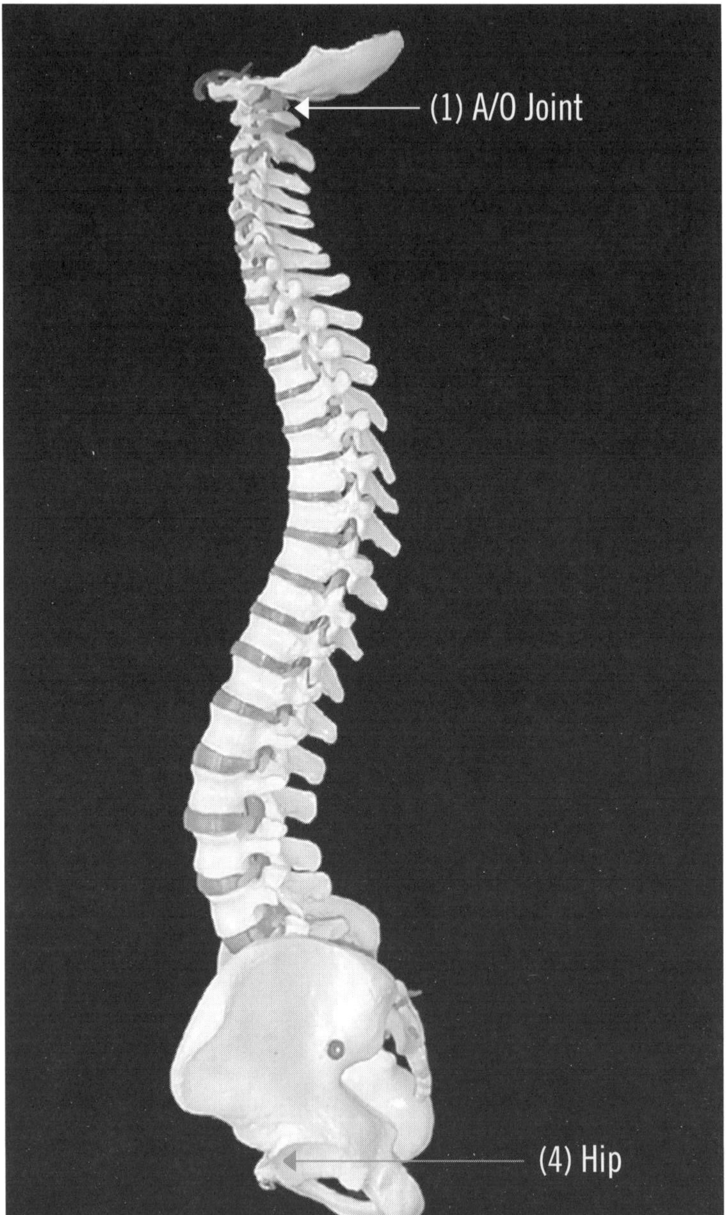

Figure 7: Spinal column (side view) from A/O joint to pelvis

Figure 8: Incorrect use of the Swiss Ball: perching and "holding" the weight of the body with the legs

Figure 9: Correct use of the Swiss Ball; Organizing the core of the body on the top center of the Swiss Ball using legs for balance (front view)

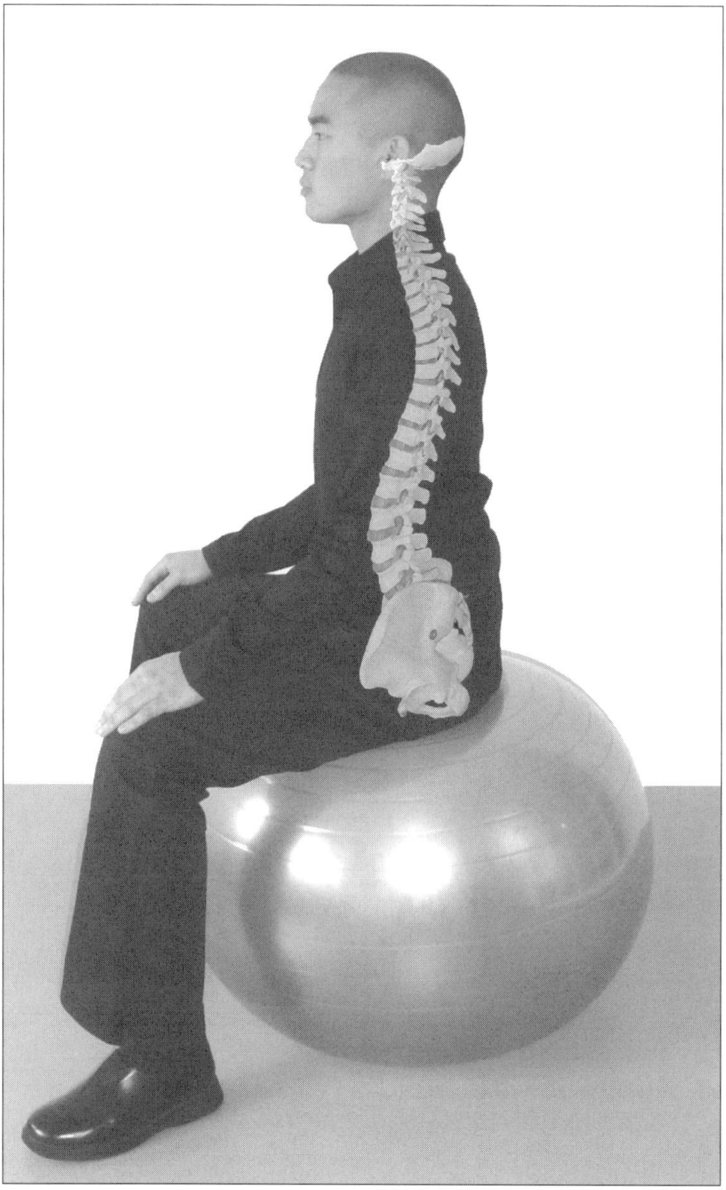

Figure 10: Correct use of the Swiss Ball; Organizing the core of the body on the top center of the Swiss Ball using legs for balance (side view)

The Organization of Your Body: Like an Apple with a Core

Many problems are created by conductors because they possess incorrect fantasies about the role of the spine and its relationship to overall alignment. Many conductors believe that their entire "erect" being is organized around a "flat back." That is, their spine can line up perfectly if they place their body against a wall. Aside from the fantasy about the A/O joint, this fantasy of a "flat back" is a great inhibitor of expressive conducting technique. The truth is that the spine is composed of two structural entities. The forward half of the spine is the weight-bearing half, providing a core for the rest of the torso, which surrounds it like an apple. **This is the weight-bearing portion of the spine.** The back portion of the spine, the bony spinal process that we can feel when we touch our backs, is the nerve-holding half of the spinal column.

Motion Generation: Fingertips Backward!

As you begin your work on the Swiss Ball, it is important to understand from which point in your arm motion is generated, produced, or initiated. The common misconception is that motion is generated from the shoulder forward. Such a misconception produces a gesture that is rigid, tight, and has limited flexibility and fluidity. Motion generated from the shoulder also does not utilize efficient, free, and effortless movement of the arm.

Arm motion is generated for the entire arm from the fingertips backward. The logic of this is not hard to see. If you were asked to pick up a pencil from a table, I doubt whether you would thrust your shoulder forward toward the pencil.

Rather, it is more likely that you would reach toward the pencil, fingertips leading the movement back through all four joints of the arm. Movement conceptualized in such a way allows for a gesture devoid of tension.

Map Yourself for Size

Most musicians have not mapped themselves for size. Our Body Map constantly changes as we gain weight, lose weight, and grow taller. Many who have experienced growth spurts in their teen years never remap their bodies for their new size. That is, if they are now 6' 2", they may conduct as if they were 5'8", the height they were before the growth spurt. Larger bodies must use more physical space to move and smaller ones, obviously, use less. However, the use of that space is based totally on one's self-perception of his or her body. It is important that you have made decisions about the size of your Body Map before you begin your conducting work. Stated in another way, if you are taller, you need to make sure that you are using gestures that are size-appropriate. Longer arms need more space to move well. When people who have mis-mapped themselves as smaller first try to "open-up" they feel that their gestures are themselves "too big." This is due to the fact that such persons have under-utilized movement space. When they try a larger gesture it feels "uncomfortable." It will feel that way because it is a new sensation in their inclusive awareness. In such cases, it is important to use a mirror for visual feedback. If the gesture looks too large, it probably is. Adjust gestural size when it seems visually appropriate to you.

Building All Conducting Technique from the Embrace

There are many approaches for the teaching of conducting.

There are, likewise, many approaches to the "starting" or "beginning" body position for conductors. Given the Body Mapping material presented on the *Evoking Sound* video, it seems obvious that the most efficient and free movement is generated from a home position from both hands and arms that reflects an embrace. The justification for this from a human point of view is obvious. The "beginning" hand position should be one that resembles a handshake. This is the most normal and relaxed position for the hand. Although the patterns employed for conducting may grow larger or smaller depending on dynamics and musical intent, the circumference of the embrace should never be compromised. By learning conducting technique on the Swiss Ball, you are less likely to experience a collapse of this space. Remember that when the arms are in the appropriate embracing position, there will be space under each of the arms. For maximum use of the arm, this space must be maintained.

Use of Mirrors

While using the Swiss Ball for technique practice and development, it is most beneficial if a mirror could be used both privately and in class for immediate visual feedback for each conductor. Self-monitoring of errors in body usage can be extremely beneficial for the overall progress of conducting technique. Constant evaluation of body usage with mirrors allows for almost instantaneous correction of problems that may occur.

Figure 11: Embracing anticipatory position with appropriate relationship of arm to body

Figure 12: Embracing anticipatory position with improper "collapsed" space between arm and body cavity

Location of Axes

The hands move and the arms follow based upon an axis location for each of the arms. Many approaches to conducting teach that all conducting patterns are organized around a singular perpendicular that is located in the exact center of the body. While this may seem logical, it is illogical if one considers what constitutes correct and efficient movement of the arms. Placing beat one of every pattern on the center of the body immediately limits the range of motion possible in each limb, which compromises freedom of movement and free rotation. When this motion is compromised, the reduced range of motion usually transfers in some way to the core of the body. Many conductors who use their arms without respect to correct axis location soon find that some, if not all, of their six points of balance are compromised. When each arm works off each respective axis as one sits on the Swiss Ball, movement of the arm is always kinesthetically learned in constant relationship to the core of the body!

There is a vertical axis for each hand. In males, the axes of the right and left hands is a few inches outward from the core of the body in a slightly interior direction from the shoulder blade. In women, the axes will be slightly wider. In the case of male and female, the location of these vertical axes is a reflection of one's Body Map for body size and type. Each hand works off its own axis as conducting patterns are learned.

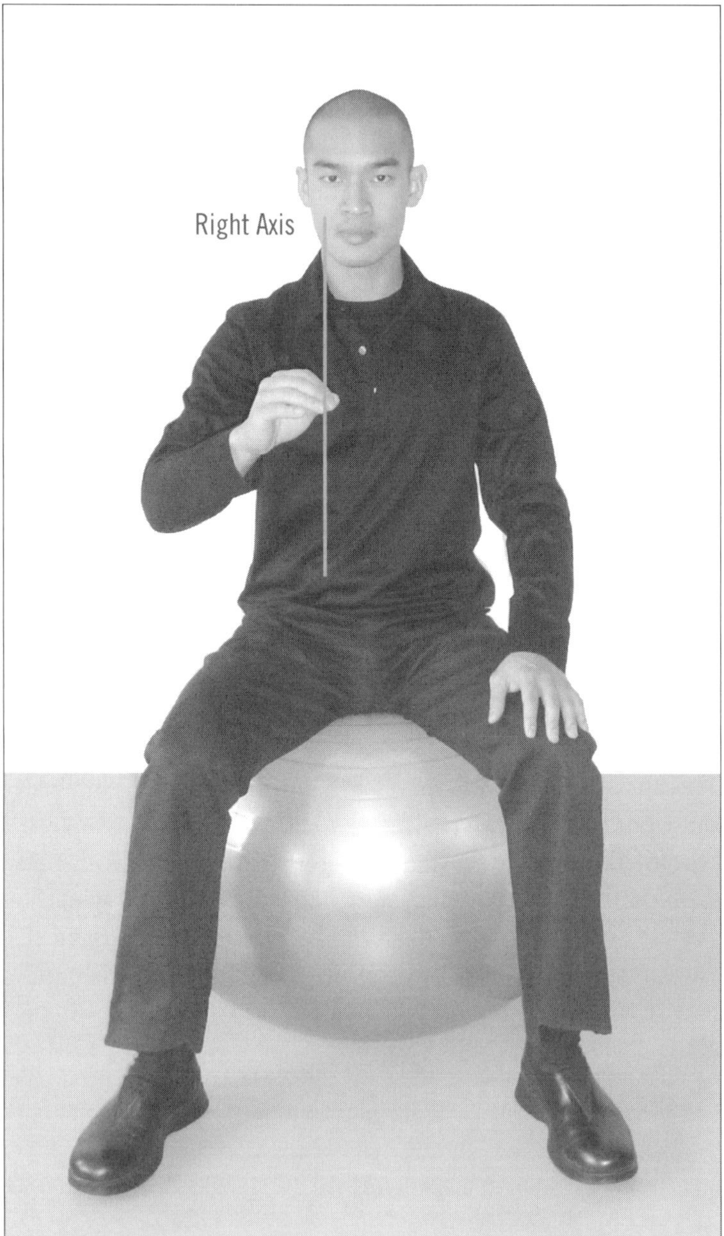

Figure 13: Location of axis for right hand and arm

Figure 14: Location of axis for left hand and arm

The Embrace: The Beginning Position for All Conducting Gestures

The starting, beginning, or anticipatory position for a conductor is probably one of the most important aspects of conducting. The use of the Swiss Ball helps to connect the hand and arm position with the core of the body. If the body is organized around its core, each arm, working off its axis, assumes a rounded position that exactly mirrors the embrace of another person. This attitude places the arms and hands in a position that allows for free and unencumbered movement.

While the following point may be controversial, I would ask you to answer which position of the hand allows for maximum movement potential of the arm and relates directly to a correct Body Map of one's arms and hands.

The hands should assume a handshaking position as a "home" position. In relationship to the floor, hands should be more perpendicular rather than parallel. Such a hand position organizes the hand more around the ulna. The handshake position also engenders and evokes a more welcoming and humane non-verbal message to the choir. Sitting on the Swiss Ball, place your hands and arms in a welcoming embrace. Feel the relationship of your hands to the core of your body as you sit on the ball. You may want to check your anticipatory position in the mirror. The elbow joint should feel rounded and not angular. The arms should be at an approximate 45-degree angle with the core of the body and the body cavity.

Figure 15: Beginning anticipatory position from front using the Swiss Ball

Figure 16: Beginning anticipatory position from side using the Swiss Ball

The **anticipatory position** is so called because it anticipates the receiving of sound from the ensemble. This position is not only an issue of correct alignment, but one of spiritual openness and acceptance. Creating that "openness" (to receive their sound) in addition to breath coming into the body, is the part of conducting that transforms it from mere time beating to artistry. Whether you are a church choir director or a college conductor, the same principles apply. Many conducting texts first teach technique (i.e., the movement of the limbs to specific geometric patterns). The preparation, as it were, of the "inside" of the person is not dealt with. The preparation of the "inside" of the conductor is known only to those conductors who rise to the highest levels of the profession. The reality is that this element of "openness" of "receiving the sound" is the starting point for the development of all conducting and communication. Without opening yourself to the human beings with whom you are about to work, connection to them is impossible at the most basic of levels: person communicating with another person. Without that connection, spontaneous music making that is manifested by color, line, rhythm, and spirit is impossible. From the onset, conducting must be from the inside out rather than from the outside in.

What does this "inside-out" feel like? Imagine that you have just spent many weeks shopping for a special present for the most important person in your life. You have purchased it early and have been keeping it secret for many months. The day finally arrives for you to give it to this person. What is your feeling as you present this special gift to them? What is that "inside" feeling that you feel when you are about to share and give something to another person you admire? It is not only the feeling that comes from inside you but the almost instantaneous receiving of that person's innermost feelings—all wordless and unspoken.

Imagine another life situation. You are waiting at the train station for someone you have not seen for some time and for whom you have great admiration. You wait patiently on the train platform for him or her. The train stops. The doors open. You quickly scan the platform for the person among hundreds of heads. You suddenly see the person and run toward him or her with arms outstretched. Your body opens in an embrace. What does your "inside" feel like during this welcome, and what do you feel as he or she welcomes you?

It would indeed be foolish to try to put into words those feelings from the above scenes. Language simply falls short in trying to express what our "inside" feels in such situations. But know that each time you rehearse with your choir, you must be able to shed the baggage of the week, the day, or the previous hour. You must be able, prior to singing, to open your body in similar fashion to the above scenarios. The ability to do this will open the door to music making at its highest levels. To avoid openness or not to ponder its effect upon music making is to ignore one of the major tenets of artistic conducting: openness to the ensemble.

There is yet one other "state of mind" that is desirable to have in place for music making to begin. Can you recall your earliest childhood play experience? It can be an experience alone or with others. Try to recall the happiest of times. You can, no doubt, recall not only the specific situation, but the "feeling" of the situation. The ideal play is that play which has no rules, no boundaries. It is timeless. One is almost virtually unaware of the surrounding world, for one creates a world unto itself where one is totally immersed in the activity at hand. Can you place yourself there again? To validate your experience, spend some time observing children at a local playground or daycare center. The spirit of play and spontaneity of childhood is the same spontaneity and spirit of music making. Whether it is as a conductor or performer, that childlike, innocent state is necessary for music to speak clearly through us to others.

These two "inside" states—the welcoming, caring state and the play state—must be recreated as one begins a piece of music. To do otherwise produces a product much less musical and much less human. It is hard to imagine a childhood without play. It is hard to imagine a life without other human beings. It should be, likewise, impossible for conductors to begin with their choir until they are able to allow their "inside" to reflect those qualities so that their choir can, in turn, reflect their conductor. Conducting, then, is very much like a mirror image of oneself, a reflection of the inside manifest in sound. That manifestation of sound begins with the preparation of the proper spirit for music making to establish itself through the attitude of the body, both physically and spiritually.

Development of Kinesthetic Memory: Kinclusive Awareness

> Alexander's work can do much more than help overcome painful body problems for the performer. It can bring the performer's body under more conscious control and therefore increase its versatility as an instrument for artistic expression.
>
> Conductors can get better results from their orchestras because they are more in touch with the way they use energy in their bodies. (p. 184)
>
> Deborah Caplan
> *Back Trouble: A New Approach to Prevention and Recovery*

It is my opinion that in some conducting pedagogies, when arm "motion" was learned in a state of kinesthetic unawareness of the entire body, patterns appear to the ensemble as "detached" from the human being who is executing them. Moreover, people "lose" conducting patterns when they stop listening OR become kinesthetically unaware of the pattern.

If patterns are learned sitting on the Swiss Ball, then one always learns patterns in a state of inclusive awareness that includes and integrates the core of the body into one's awareness of the pattern and its "feeling" as it is executed in an organic relationship to the core of the body at all times. Repeated practice on the Swiss Ball keeps one in a constant state of awareness. Hence pattern and body are bound inclusively into one's kinesthetic memory. Kinesthetic memory is one of the important tools for a conductor. Kinclusive awareness is a term coined to describe the bonding of kinesthesia of movement through space with one's arms to the core of the body. Kinclusive awareness describes movement that is learned in synchronicity with the core of the body with the simultaneous sound of music. Stated in another way, one should never learn conducting movement separately from the core of the body and without the presence of sound.

Therein lies the miracle of the Swiss Ball! By using the Swiss Ball consistently over a long period of technique development and/or technique repair (for experienced conductors), this kinclusive awareness becomes the norm of "feeling" for the conductor. When such a kinclusive awareness is in place, it is relatively easy to connect musical ideas to one's body, which then communicates musical ideas to the ensemble. Movement is always learned in context and in awareness with the core of the body and sound!

Use of Constant Exhalation During Conducting

One of the most valuable techniques for a conductor is the use of constant exhalation. That is, when one is either conducting or practicing conducting, one should lightly exhale, similar to the breath flow used in fogging a window. The mouth should remain open at all times, and the air supply should be replenished as needed.

Two examples from other disciplines support the argument for constant exhalation by conductors. In the field of dance, dancers are taught to inhale as they begin to move and to exhale as they move. Exhalation occurs constantly as they move. If exhalation does not occur, the movements of the dancer become rigid and less fluid, and it then becomes increasingly more difficult to allow the body to move in a natural and unencumbered response to rhythm. Without the body-air exchange, muscles begin to lock because of a lack of oxygen to the muscles, and spontaneous movement becomes more difficult. The same is true for conductors. Because conducting is body movement, conductors should constantly exhale and release their own breath **into** the sound of the ensemble.

In the field of medicine, the remarkable coordination of the respiratory system to the cardiopulmonary system is a source of fascination. The rate of respiration impacts the heart rate. There is an unseen connection between the human heartbeat and the rhythmic pulse within our musical bodies. Breath influences heart rate, heart rate directly influences rhythmic pulse, and rhythmic pulse then manifests in our conducting gestures through the released ictus. Consequently, the breath becomes the beginning and the end of music making because it connects us to our bodies, and our bodies connect us to music. It is that connection, shared with others, that then allows us to connect with them and make music together.

It follows then that one should constantly exhale while conducting to exchange air to ensure freedom of movement and natural rhythmic response. A failure to exhale while conducting will most likely result in a "locking" of the muscles and lead to a tense, arrhythmic conducting gesture that will directly affect both sound and musical line. Without constant exhalation on the part of the conductor, singers and players WILL subconsciously and technically have a more difficult time playing, singing, and producing a free sound.

Making Sound as One Develops Conducting Technique

> How vague the general concept of conducting is was brought home to me in a letter from a record buff who fancied himself a born *chef d'orchestre,* though he admitted never having studied music. From his resume, I visualized my correspondent spending many hours cutting a graceful figure in front of his speakers as the glorious strains poured from the magic machine. Many students have practiced baton technique in such a manner, but this gentleman had come to believe that his choreography was actually the cause of the wondrous beauty sounded forth. He was convinced, moreover, that he could produce the same results with a group of musicians on a public platform. Not for a moment did I consider the man deranged. He has merely confused cause and effect, as many do when they try to imagine the task of the musical conductor. Anyone with some musical instinct can follow the outlines of a symphony with appropriately synchronized gestures and create the illusion that the follower is the leader. (p. 167)
>
> Erich Leinsdorf
> *The Composer's Advocate*

One of the mistakes that I feel is made in the study of conducting is the notion that gesture is learned devoid of sound. A conducting gesture learned in silence will not elicit the desired musical response because it was learned without a connection to sound. The bonding of sound with gesture must take place from the very beginning of conducting study. Those who may have learned conducting gestures in this fashion can relearn them on the Swiss Ball. Simply using familiar gestures while seated on the Swiss Ball and making a sound can accomplish that goal. Sound then acts as a bonding agent to gesture. Without "sound bonding," there can be no connection to the primal elements of musical line.

My recommendation is to moan or speak neutral syllables that reflect the musical style of the gesture you are attempting to learn. In the beginning of conducting study, or in your attempt to rejuvenate older or practiced technique, you should employ spoken syllables on a monotone that reflects the musical style you are attempting to evoke through your gesture. Some guidelines for such syllables follow. Remember that syllables must be constructed that will mirror not only the musical style but also each beat and its first subdivision (macro and micro beat).

	Macro Beat Syllable	Micro Beat Syllable
Legato	"no"	"nee"
Marcato	"dah" "de" "du"	"noo" "noo" "nee"
Staccato	"tee"	"too"

The Breath Impulse Gesture: Response of the Swiss Ball

The first "ictus" in this approach to conducting is known as the breath impulse gesture. The first ictus, or the breath impulse gesture, relays the tempo, effect, color, dynamic, and line of the piece to be sung. All these necessary performance elements are relayed in the breath of the conductor.

The breath impulse gesture is, perhaps, one of the most valuable tools at the disposal of the conductor. The breath impulse gesture, as its name implies, spontaneously tells the choir to "breathe now." In many conducting texts, this is often called the preparation gesture, or simply the preparation. This gesture is often done without a direct connection to the breathing mechanism. The breath impulse gesture signals the choir to open their bodies so that air may fall in. The easiest route to understanding the breath impulse gesture is to experience it.

Find the anticipatory position. Drop your hands straight down, and when they hit "bottom" (somewhere in the vicinity of your navel), allow air to fall into your body. You may want to think of the sensation of breathing you experience when suddenly scared by a friend. When spontaneously startled, the body instinctively drops open so that breath falls into it quickly and silently. The breath seemingly drops low into the body. At the point at which the gesture hits bottom and air enters into the body, the hands instinctively move in the opposite direction, upward and slightly outward, creating a "vee" pattern. (For further clarification, see figure 8.11 in the *Evoking Sound* conducting text.)

Holding and the Line of Ictus

It is important at this point in your study to be vigilant about "holding" and the line of ictus. The use of the Swiss

Ball many times will eliminate muscular holding issues. Holding can be best demonstrated by the following example. Stand up and pick up a briefcase. Place it back on the floor and pick it up a second time. As you pick it up the second time, be sensitive to the sensation in your arms and upper body. Pick up the briefcase a third time, but this time use only the minimum of muscular effort necessary. Notice that you can pick up the same briefcase with much less muscular effort! The difference between the first time you picked up the briefcase and the last time amounts to an excess of muscular involvement. This overexertion and excess muscle activity can be labeled as holding, or locking. When performing the "vee" pattern drills above to feel the impulse gesture in conjunction with the breath, you should not "feel" your arms, elbows, or shoulders. The fingertips of the third finger of both of your hands should "feel" an imaginary dabbing sensation, but your arms should not be felt. Continuous motion of the arms is the goal, free, without feeling weighed down.

When your body is in the anticipatory position, your hands are above the actual location of your ictus. Remembering to keep your forearms relatively parallel (in a 45-degree relationship to both floor and body) to the floor in an embracing position, allow your body to open and breathe, releasing your arms into a free fall. Again, the line of ictus must be maintained; your breath should then fall into your body at the point of ictus. When done correctly, one will receive feedback from the Swiss Ball in the form of a slight bounce or recoil.

Rebound and Release: More Feedback from the Swiss Ball

The Released Rebound Gesture. An axiom of physics states that for every action there is an equal and opposite reaction.

As the arm drops to the point at which an ictus manifests (at waist level), *the forearm is parallel to the floor* and the forearm is never at a higher level than the upper arm. After the ictus, the arm instantaneously rebounds in the opposite direction and toward the outside. What must be understood, however, is that the rebound upward is not at the same speed as the descent of the hand-arm unit. *Moreover, the hand on the rebound never reaches the full height from which it dropped.* In reality, the conductor must wait for the rebound to occur. The sensation of a correct rebound is that it moves more slowly than the descent to the point of ictus.

Some comparisons to real life experiences might be helpful at this point. When you throw a rubber ball to the ground, the force of your downward throw gains momentum because the ball is moving with gravity. When the ball hits the ground (similar to an ictus), the ball changes direction and bounces upward. The ascent of the ball is *slower* than its descent because it is now moving against gravity. *The ball also does not return to the level from which it was dropped.* The action (throwing) and reaction (bouncing) of the ball are identical in approach to the ictus and the rebound. When the hand-arm drops toward the point of ictus, the muscles in the arm should be released so that it engages in a free fall. When the ictus occurs, many novice conductors *make* their arms rebound upward at the same rate of speed as the descent, and the same distance is covered in both directions. In actuality, just like the bouncing ball, *the rebound or ascent will be slower than the descent.* The conductor must wait and allow the rebound to occur naturally. The correct sensation is that the rebound is slower than the descent to the ictus. To do otherwise creates an upward motion that is equal in intensity to the downward motion through muscular involvement of the forearm. This upward moving gesture runs the risk of becoming a subdivision, which will in turn slow the tempo and impede the natural forward movement of the line. The seemingly slower rebound is known as a released gesture because the musculature of the arm does not inhibit the natural upward motion of the arm.

Learning Baton Technique on the Swiss Ball

It is a simple matter to transfer what has already been learned to the baton. *A cautionary note:* It is recommended that conducting technique begin without a baton. Awareness for correct movement should be developed using just the natural parts of the body. Introducing a baton prematurely may inhibit correct usage. Once basic technique has been developed on the Swiss Ball, then one can proceed to add the baton to the hand.

The holding of the baton should make use of a hand position that allows for free ulnar rotation and humero-scapular rotation as demonstrated on the *Evoking Sound* video. A correct hand position is one that utilizes ulnar freedom, rather than reliance on radial movement of the arm. Many conducting grips inadvertently emphasize the radius bone of the arm, which will severely limit conducting technique and may lead to physical pain and damage. The baton should be grasped as if one is shaking another's hand. This is the most natural use of the hand and allows for maximum freedom of movement.

Figure 17: Incorrect "home" position for baton

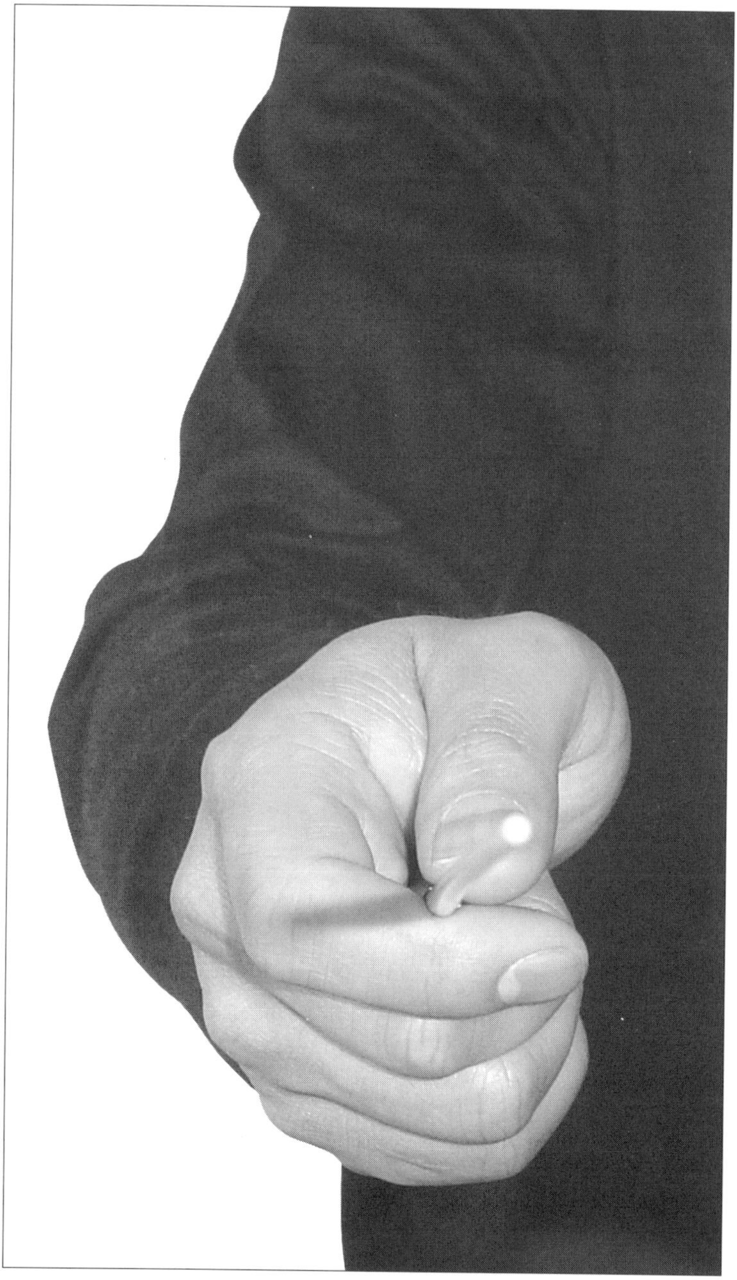

Figure 18: Correct "home" position for baton

Remedial Baton Grip Therapy: First Aid for Conductors

If you are unsure if you are maximizing good ulnar usage OR if you have used a different grip than described here, you should review all styles of conducting patterns using a "remedial grip." Hold the baton with the thumb and the little finger. By holding the baton in this way, you will be reorganizing your arm around the ulna rather than the radius. A signal that a conductor is organized improperly around his or her radius is the dominance of thumb usage in the conducting gesture either with thumb tension OR an upward-pointing thumb. For those who have had technique built around a radius, holding the baton with the little finger and thumb will feel VERY different. Different is good! Repeated drill and practice will teach the new "feeling" and make it part of your kinesthetic vocabulary. If you are unclear on the role of the ulna and radius in conducting gestures, you are mis-mapped. Watch the arm section of the *Evoking Sound* conducting video again.

Use of Rattles for Learning Marcato and Staccato on the Swiss Ball

Many times, both beginning and advanced students have difficulty exhibiting a clear ictus, especially in dealing with marcato and staccato textures. (For a definition of ictus, see the *Evoking Sound* conducting text.) Gestural problems range from avoiding the ictus to muscular "locking" or rigidity after the ictus. Many times, this rigidity occurs in part because the gesture is produced apart from the core of the body, thereby compromising the alignment of the core of the body. The use of the Swiss Ball gives appropriate and immediate kinclusive awareness feedback to the conductor. In most cases, if the body alignment is correct, and if the arm is dropping straight down and up (keeping in mind the line of ictus), the ictus may not speak because the muscles in the arm are too involved with the rebound gesture.

A drill to remove unnecessary muscular tension from the rebound (and also from the drop to the ictus) is to find either a small, traditional baby rattle (sometimes marketed as "chikitas" in the percussion world) with a round top and straight handle that is approximately three inches in length, or a set of maracas available in most toy stores. Grasp and encircle your hand and wrist around the egg-shaped portion of the rattle with your wrist. NOTE: Make sure you have your wrist correctly mapped!. Your wrist is actually the collection of carpal bones associated with the palm of your hand.

Shake the rattle and get it to speak in a clean, staccato sound. The rattle will only speak when excess muscular effort is removed from the arm. *Be certain to have space between your upper arm and body.* A lack of space will inhibit the natural movement of the arm. If there is muscular effort in the arm, the sound-producing beads in the rattle will either double the sound or not sound at all. After you have discovered how to make the rattle speak in a staccato fashion, hold the rattle and speak the repeated syllable "tee," breathing before every series of "tees." A clean shake sound should occur at the same time you speak "tee." You will find that when the drop and rebound are correct, the rattle speaks effortlessly. You will also discover that when this is executed correctly, there is a **slight** "bounce" or "recoil" on the Swiss Ball! If you use too much weight in getting the rattle to shake, you will get something closer to a marcato sound. Hence, the recoil in the Swiss Ball will be more pronounced.

Marcato. Perform the same exercise as above, this time substituting the *forte* word "dah" for the *forte* word "tee." Breathe and speak seven forte "dahs." When you breathe, the breath should go deep into your pelvis, well below your navel. *Listen to the sound that you produce.* Describe the intensity and quality of that *forte* marcato sound. The marcato sound is characterized by a rhythmic thrust behind the sound followed by a decay of the sound. Perform the marcato "dah" exercise again, this time making note of the thrust and decay of the sound that defines a marcato articulation. Notice how your arm moves upward on the breath with the predominant motion through the entire arm, beginning with the fingertips and moving through the arm all the way through to the sterno-clavicular joint. Your arm then drops straight down in a free fall without any muscular holding. The entire arm falls straight down and rebounds straight up. If you find yourself skimming the beat (avoiding the ictus or bypassing the ictus), hold your left forearm out in front of you. Speak the word "dah," and drop your right forearm on your left forearm. In marcato, you will notice that your right forearm thrusts into your left forearm. Feel the release of your arms straight upward after the marcato is articulated.

The Swiss Ball can provide two types of kinclusive feedback for marcato. First, when marcato is executed while sitting on the Swiss Ball, a pronounced bounce will be experienced for each marcato beat IF the core of the body is correctly aligned and lengthened. If one does not experience this "bounce," the problem most likely is an improper alignment of the arm and use of the arms on their respective axis.

To correct this common technical problem, kneel with the Swiss Ball in front of you. Using your dominant hand and arm, drop your entire arm onto the Swiss Ball, contacting the Swiss Ball with the radial/ulna portion of your arm. Your "forearm" should contact the ball and then be repelled away from the ball naturally. You should NOT pull your arm upward on the rebound. When done correctly, you will feel as if no work is being done. It is important speak the syllable "dah" each time the arm contacts the Swiss Ball. After experiencing this, sit again on the Swiss Ball and recall the kinclusive awareness that you had just learned from the kneeling position. The Swiss Ball should provide a "bouncing" feedback when used correctly! Remember to maintain length between points 1 and 4 (hips, lumbar vertebrae, and A/O joint)!

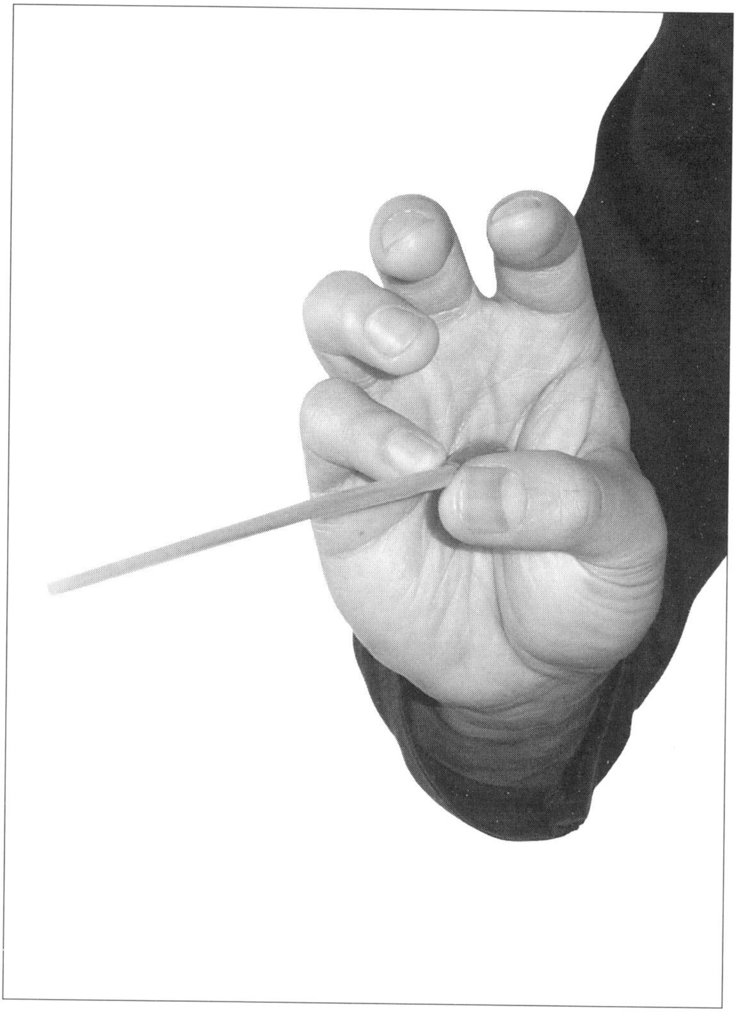

Figure 19: Remedial "thumb/little finger" grip to correct baton grip problems

Figure 20: Correct holding position for "chickita" rattle

Figure 21: Beginning position using the Swiss Ball for learning kinclusive awareness and correct arm/hand usage and relationship for staccato and marcato

Figure 22: Contact of "forearm" with Swiss Ball to learn released rebound sensation

Arm Rotation: The Key to Expressive Conducting

One of the most severe problems in conductors is the fact that they do not understand that there are three rotations available in the arm structure and all are needed for the art of conducting. Freedom gained in the fluid use of these rotations will release sound from the ensemble. (For detailed and further explanations, consult the *Evoking Sound* video and *What Every Musician Needs to Know About the Body*). To assist this process, a beautifully clear illustration of the three rotations of the arm from that text are reprinted on page 85.

Specific Drills for Maximizing Arm Usage After Remapping

There are two exercises that I feel expand the range of movement capable with the arm and hand in a relatively easy fashion. Those exercises are repetitive movement patterns that use swimming gestures and "arm-flapping" gestures. Both of these exercises have the effect of correctly establishing conducting technique in new conductors and correcting poor usage and technique in more experienced conductors.

Swimming Gesture: Releasing the Sterno-clavicular Joint

On the Evoking Sound video, particular attention should be paid to the section concerning the arm structure and how it moves. On that video, a pivotal piece of information is given that will unlock free movement in the arms. There are FOUR joints: (1) behind the hand, (2) at the elbow, (3) the "shoulder," and (4) the joint that connects and pivots the collarbone at the sternum! Many conductors simply do not realize that the collarbone is a part of the arm, and because they don't envision it as part of the arm, they do not employ it in the movement of their arm! The use of a "swimming" gesture can quickly re-engage the collarbone to the rest of the arm!

Sitting correctly on the Swiss Ball, move the arms in a repeated swimming gesture. After doing several repetitions, move immediately to the conducting pattern that you are working on. Remember always to move from the swimming movement to the conducting pattern. This movement causes one to use all joints of the arms, especially the sterno-clavicular joint as discussed on the *Evoking Sound* video.

Winged Gesture Exercise

The upper arm leading to the sterno-clavicular joint is often the portion of the arm that is both under-utilized by conductors and carries the greatest amount of tension for the conductor. This exercise tends to free the upper arm. Take your fingertips and place them on your sterno-clavicular joint. Slowly rotate your arms in a repeated circular pattern.

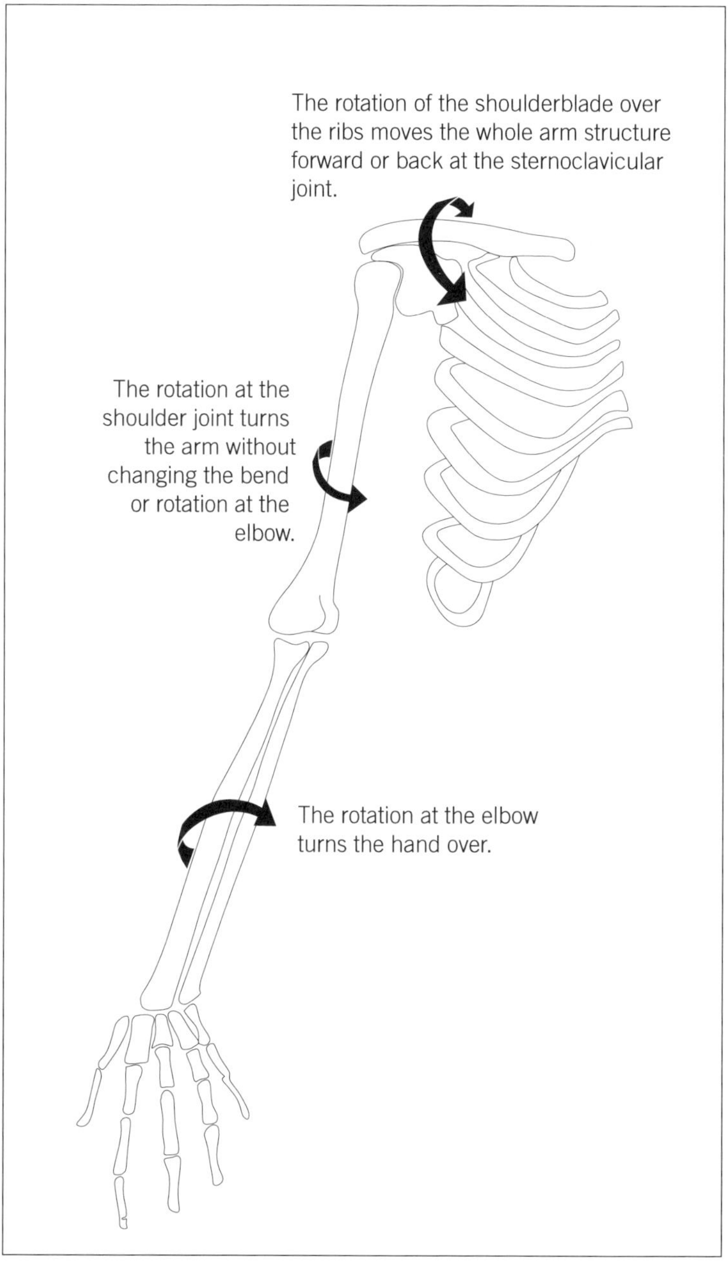

Figure 23: The three rotations of the arm

Figure 24: Swimming gesture on the Swiss Ball

Figure 25: Winged gesture exercise (top position)

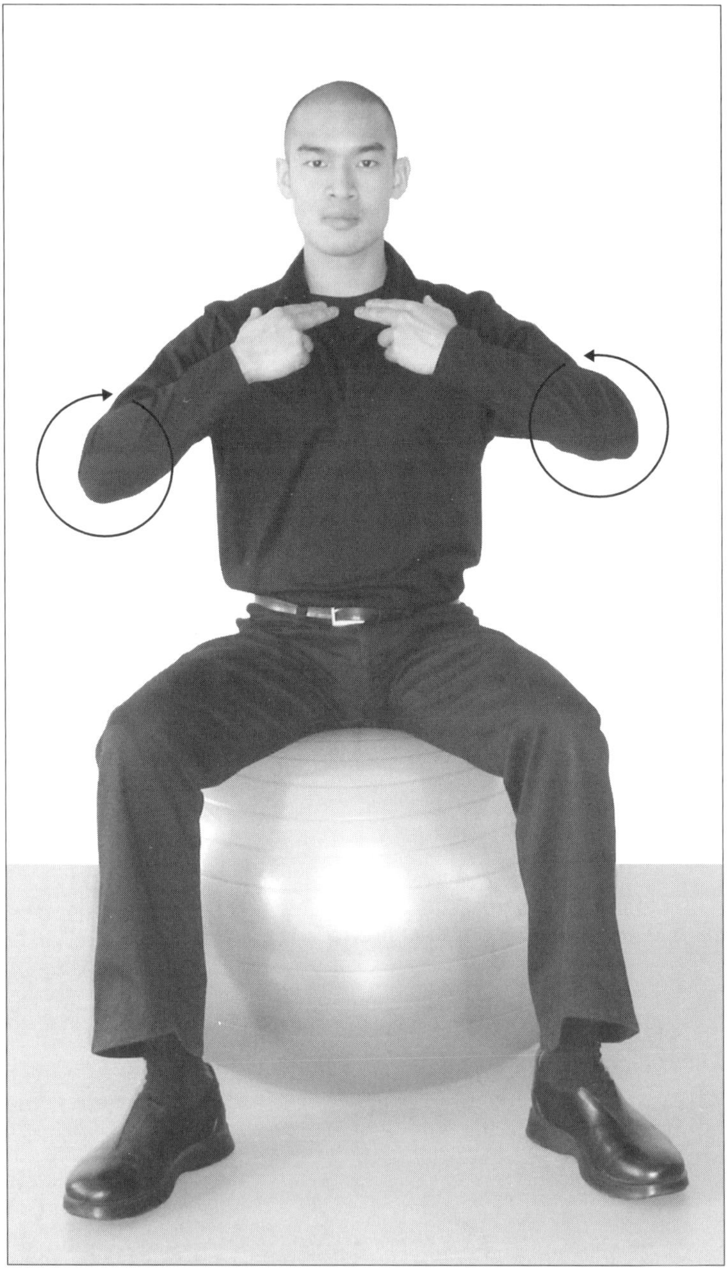

Figure 26: Winged gesture (bottom position)

A Word on Conducting Patterns

There are many approaches to the "geometry" of conducting patterns. My approach for the teaching of basic conducting patterns is contained in the second portion of the video *Evoking Sound.* All approaches to the geometry of patterns can be effectively taught using the Swiss Ball.

Always Practice Old and Learn New Technique

No matter what approach is taken to specific patterns, it is important to always "input" new conducting patterns while seated on the Swiss Ball. In initial stages of conducting instruction or when one is trying to refurbish older conducting technique, practice of patterns should only take place when one is on the Swiss Ball. Practicing off the Swiss Ball will compromise both alignment and overall awareness. The beauty of the Swiss Ball is that there is an immediate bonding of pattern with kinclusive awareness. Patterns are then always learned with the core of the body intact!

The Use of the Swiss Exercise Ball in the Conducting Class

It is recommended that there be an appropriately sized Swiss Ball for each student in the conducting class. Once Body Mapping principles on the *Evoking Sound* video have been taught, all technique should be practiced on the Swiss Ball. It is also important that students sit on the Swiss Exercise Balls throughout the semester. The reason for this is relatively simple. If you allow students to return to traditional classroom chairs, movement to those chairs will cause them to lose awareness concerning their bodies. Then, when it is time for a student to conduct in class, it is difficult, if not impossible, for the student to "find" their correct alignment quickly. Moreover, they will probably bring the unawareness that was encouraged by poor classroom seating to their conducting. When the Swiss Ball is used during all instructional periods, I have found that correct alignment becomes second nature and free, and expressive conducting is the result.

A Technical Warm-up Sequence Using the Swiss Ball

For each conducting class or conducting session, there should be a consistent "warm-up" session that allows one to acclimate oneself to a heightened state of kinclusive awareness. This period should be no less than five minutes in duration. The following elements should be used for each session:

(1) **Body Drape.** Students should drape over the balls for a period of constructive rest at the beginning of class. This should be at least three to five minutes. No talking should take place. A quiet room is optimal for this constructive rest time. In addition to the psychological benefits of this constructive rest time, ball draping allows for a gradual lengthening of the spine, ridding the conductor of alignment tensions brought to the class from his or her daily life. It is suggested that meditative music be played during this time. Suggested music can be found in the bibliography of this book.

(2) **Exhalation and Inhalation.** The students should sit on their Swiss Ball and simply exhale and inhale for a period not less than one minute.

(3) **Rotation Freeing Exercises.** Because movement of the arms during the day may underutilize rotations that are needed for the arms in conducting, it is important to perform

several repetitions of both the "swimming" movement and the "winged" movements while seated on the Swiss Ball.

(4) **Technical Review: Keeping Kinclusive Awareness Alive.** After initial conducting technique has been taught, it is necessary to review that technique at the beginning of each class session to keep the kinclusive awareness alive and to preempt the invasion of poor technique into the conductor's vocabulary! It is during this period that new technical elements should be taught and reviewed. Use mirrors whenever possible to reinforce good movement.

(5) **Class Conducting Awareness.** Do not be afraid to have the student conduct on the Swiss Ball in front of the class when any Body Mapping difficulty regarding good usage or a technical problem appears. Be careful not to explain or physically manipulate the conductor's arms because that pedagogical process will bypass and short-circuit body awareness and undermine the kinclusive awareness that one has worked to build within each conductor. After he or she conducts on the Swiss Ball, immediately have the conductor repeat the performance, focusing upon listening to the music AND listening to his or her body in the same way as when sitting on the Swiss Ball.

Making the Transition from the Swiss Ball to "Standing" Conducting

The transition from instruction and drill sitting on the Swiss Ball to standing conducting should be relatively simple, as long as you keep several points in mind. Make sure that the students have their legs and feet correctly mapped! (See the *Evoking Sound* video.) Make certain that weight is distributed on three points in each foot and that the knees are released, but not locked.

The biggest dangers coming off the Swiss Ball are that (1) students may quickly lose awareness of their legs and feet and begin to lose the kinclusive awareness of being organized around their core and (2) they will not lead with their head upward as they stand. Instead they thrust their bodies upward, detaching from their core. Simple verbal reminders can often cue necessary kinclusive awareness. The instructor should make evaluations of conducting, first focusing on body organization and Body Mapping issues. After feedback and reinforcement are given to the student, musical matters can then be dealt with. Always correct Body Mapping issues first, and return to the Swiss Ball whenever necessary to regain kinclusive awareness.

Verbal "Self-Cues" to Maintain Alignment Awareness

In addition to feedback directly from the Swiss Ball, you can also correct conducting technique through use of verbal cues to yourself as you kinesthetically acquire conducting technique. In addition to using the feedback of a mirror, it is very helpful to use verbal cues to maintain oneself in a state of constant awareness. Never underestimate the power of verbal cues to maintain the necessary state of inclusive awareness. The danger for conductors is reducing their level of kinclusive awareness as they "focus" upon gesture. The use of simple verbal "self-reminders" are powerful and sufficient gauges to maintain inclusive awareness. I would suggest that the reminders below be written on a 5X7 card and kept within sight as one works on the Swiss Ball. Practice sessions should be periodically interrupted to use the alignment cues as "checks" on the degree of inclusive awareness.

Verbal Alignment Cues for Conducting Practice

- Conduct with your whole body.
- Are you keeping your head independent and mobile?
- Are you thinking up and over?
- Is the joint connecting your head to your spine free? Can you sense it?
- Remember your weight-bearing spine, at your core.
- Are you balanced at your hip joints?
- Are your knees released and flexible?
- Are your feet feeling the floor?
- Are you feeling the tripod of your feet's arches?
- Is your head dynamically poised?
- Is your back free? Long and wide?
- Remember to organize around your spine like an apple around a core.
- When you look at your music, just tilt your head. Don't drag your head forward.
- Remember to balance your arms. Don't pull them back, or slump them down.
- Are you aware of all the skin covering your body?
- Are you aware of your wrist?
- Is all your motion generated from your fingertips backward?
- Are you aware of your back as you conduct?

Figure 27: Standing alignment transferred from Swiss Ball

Conclusions

There is no doubt in my mind about the pedagogical potency of the use of the Swiss Ball for conducting study. The use of this simple device transfers responsibility for teaching from heretofore-used verbal explanations to a new world of instruction that uses body awareness as the primary vehicle for instruction. Conducting technique taught via the Swiss Ball achieves a remarkable fluidity and expressivity previously somewhat elusive during the instructional and practice period. I have altered my overall philosophy of conducting teaching to include the teaching and reinforcement of awareness: kinclusive awareness. If one is to believe that conductors should be alive human beings in front of ensembles, it follows that such aliveness can only be achieved through untraditional methods of instruction to marry one's listening, kinesthesia, and body into one coherent, vibrant being.

The Swiss Ball provides such a long-awaited vehicle! It is important to keep in mind the following list of words from *How to Learn the Alexander Technique* (p. 98), which is a "lexicon" of verbal cues that will remind one of new-found body freedom. These cues should be used to keep one in a state of awareness as one works to improve conducting technique:

comfortable	**balanced**	**freedom**
lighten	**elegant**	**luxurious**
grounded	**easy**	**supported**
feathery	**graceful**	**in contact**
firm	**effortless**	**light**

buoyant

floating facility

steady

stable

effortlessly

free

buoyancy

smooth elegance

secure

stability

rooted

Enjoy your newfound awareness courtesy of the Swiss Exercise Ball!

About the Author

James Jordan is recognized and praised from many quarters in the musical world as one of the nation's pre-eminent conductors, writers, and innovators in choral teaching. He has been called a "visionary" by *The Choral Journal*. His career and publications are devoted to innovative educational changes in the choral art and have been embraced around the world. A master teacher, Dr. Jordan's pioneering writing and research concerning the use of Laban Movement Analysis for the teaching of conducting and movement to children has dramatically changed teaching in both those disciplines. Called the "Father of the Case Study," he was the first researcher to bring forward the idea of the case study as a viable and valuable form of research for the training and education of teachers.

One of the country's most prolific writers on the subjects of the philosophy of music making and choral teaching, he has produced ten major textbooks and several choral series bearing his name. He has contributed to four other textbooks. In 2004, four new books authored by him will be published: *Learn Conducting Technique With The Swiss Exercise Ball: Developing Kinclusive Conducting Awareness*, *Ear Training Immersion Exercises For Choirs* (book, CD, and singer's edition), *Evoking Sound: Choral Warm-Up Core Vocal Exercises* (book, CD, and accompanist's edition), and *The Musician's Walk* (all published by GIA Publications, Inc., Chicago). His books on the subject of vocal technique for choirs are considered essential for the education of conductors around the world. His choral conducting book *Evoking Sound* was named as a "must read" list of six books by *The Choral Journal*. His newest book, *Ear Training Immersion Exercises for Choirs*, details the first comprehensive approach toward aural literacy for choirs using solfege and a unique system of score analysis that focuses upon what is aurally perceived by the choir. His books *The Musician's Soul* (GIA, 2000) and *The Musician's Spirit* (GIA, 2002) are acclaimed by both instrumental and choral conductors alike and have been credited with beginning a transformation in how music is taught both in ensembles and the classroom through a process of humanizing and loving.

Dr. Jordan teaches and conducts at Westminster Choir College of Rider University in Princeton, New Jersey, one of the foremost centers for the study and performance of choral music in the world, where he is an associate professor of conducting. For the past 12 years he has served as conductor of The Westminster Chapel Choir. In the fall of 2004, he will conduct one of Westminster's highly select touring choirs, a newly inaugurated ensemble, **The Westminster Williamson Voices.** This choir's mission is not only to produce choral performances and recordings at the highest levels, but to serve as an ensemble that employs unique and cutting edge approaches to choral rehearsals and performances. The ensemble will premiere significant contributions to choral literature. The Westminster Williamson Voices is also involved with educational recordings of significant educational choral literature for the next five years for GIA Publications that will culminate in the recording of approximately 200 essential pieces of choral literature.

James Jordan has been the recipient of many awards for his contributions to the profession. He was named as Distinguished Choral Scholar at The University of Alberta and was made an honorary member of Phi Mu Alpha Sinfonia in 2002 at Florida State University. The composer Morten Lauridsen dedicated a movement of his acclaimed *Mid-Winter Songs* to Dr. Jordan. This year alone, Dr. Jordan will present more than 30 keynote addresses and workshops around the world. His books and professional activities are detailed on the Web site Evokingsound.com.

List of Figures

Bibliography

Videos

Jordan, James and Heather Buchanan. *Evoking Sound Video: Body Mapping Principles and Basic Conducting Technique.* Chicago: GIA, 2002.

This video should be used in conjunction with the book. Ideally the video should be viewed and absorbed before applying technique to the Swiss Ball.

MacMurray, Alan. *Conducting from the Inside Out: Gesture and Movement.* Chicago: GIA, 2004.

This wonderful video clearly discusses conducting issues. Included in the discussion are topics such as Baton, Eye Contact, Plane, Posture, Score and Energy, Entering into Silence, the Left Hand, and Use of Space. This video is highly recommended. It is a tremendous resource for both choral conductors and instrumental conductors.

Books and Articles

Bernstein, Leonard. *Findings.* New York: Doubleday, 1982.

Cameron, Julia. *The Artist's Way: A Spiritual Path to Higher Creativity.* G.P. Putnam and Sons, 1992.

Caplan, Deborah. *Back Trouble: A New Approach to Prevention and Recovery.* Gainesville, Florida: Triad Publishing Company, 1987.

Conable, Barbara. *The Structures and Movement of Breathing: A Primer for Choirs and Choruses.* Chicago: GIA, 2000.

Conable, Barbara and Benjamin Conable. *What Every Musician Needs to Know About the Body: The Practical Application of Body Mapping & the Alexander Technique to Making Music.* Portland, Oregon: Andover Press, 1998.

Highly recommended text to be used in conjunction with this book.

Conable, Barbara and William Conable. *How to Learn The Alexander Technique: A Manual for Students.* Portland, Oregon: Andover Press, 1991.

Creager, Caroline Corning. *Therapeutic Exercises Using the Swiss Ball.* Boulder, Colorado: Executive Physical Therapy, 1994.

Damasio, Antonio R. *Descartes' Error: Emotion, Reason, and the Human Brain.* New York: HarperCollins, 1994.

Gelb, Michael. *Body Learning: An Introduction to the Alexander Technique.* New York: Henry Holt and Company, 1987.

Gelb, Michael and Tony Buzan. *Lessons From The Art Of Juggling: How to Achieve Your Full Potential in Business, Learning, and Life.* London: Aurum Press, 1998.

Gomez, Niska. "Somarhythms: Developing Somatic Awareness with Large, Inflatable Balls." *Somatics.* Spring/Summer, 1992, 12-18.

Green, Barry and W. Timothy Gallwey. *The Inner Game of Music.* New York: Doubleday, 1986.

Kucera, Maria. *Gymnastik mit dem Hupfball.* Stuttgart: Gustave Fisher Verlag, 1978.

Klein-Vogelbach, Susanne. *Therapeutic Exercises in Functional Kinetics: Analysis and Instruction of Individually Adaptable Exercises.* Germany: Springer-Verlag, 1991.

Jordan, James. *Evoking Sound.* Chicago: GIA, 1996.

Jordan, James. *The Musician's Soul.* Chicago: GIA, 2000.

Jordan, James. *The Musician's Spirit.* Chicago: GIA, 2002.

Jordan, James. *The Musician's Walk.* Chicago, GIA, 2004.

Leinsdorf, Erich. *The Composer's Advocate.* New Haven: Yale University Press, 1981.

Richards, Mary Caroline. *Centering in Pottery, Poetry, and the Person.* Middletown, Connecticut: Wesleyan University Press, 1989.

Shrock, Dennis. "An Interview with Weston Noble." *The Choral Journal,* 32, December 1991, 7-11.

Todd, Mabel E. *The Thinking Body: A Study of the Balancing Forces of Dynamic Man.* Hightstown, New Jersey: Princeton Book Company, 1937.

Suggested Recordings

Bach: The Art of Fugue. The Emerson String Quartet, Deutsche Grammophone.

Bamboo: Music for the Relaxing Arts. PC Davidoff and Friends. Available from Garland of Letters, 527 South Street, Philadelphia, PA 19147. 215-923-5946. E-mail: Om@aol.com.

The Bells of Arcosanti. Timeless Productions, 1998. Available from www.timelessproductions.com.

Buddha: Music for the Healing Arts. PC Davidoff. Available from Garland of Letters, 527 South Street, Philadelphia, PA 19147. 215-923-5946. E-mail: Om@aol.com.

Seven Metals: Singing Bowls of Tibet. Benjamin Iobst. Available from Compact Disc, PO Box 61, Orefield, PA 18069.

Web sites and Contacts

Bodymap.org. This is the Web site of Body Mapping expert Barbara Conable. Extensive information concerning workshops, certification, and related publications are listed on this site.

CarolineCreager.com. This is the Web site of Caroline Creager, who has written several books on applications of the Swiss Ball.

Evokingsound.com. Web site of James Jordan.

Alexandertechnique.com. Web site devoted to Alexander teachers and resources.

Stat.org.uk. Web site devoted to Alexander Technique in the United Kingdom.

Growthinmotion.org. Growth in Motion is a proven movement discipline created by Fanchon Shur. It is a holistic technique, which connects the body, mind, emotions, and spirit. Through movement, body awareness, and creative expression, balance and ease are created in all aspects of life.

heather@bodymapping.net. Contact for Heather Buchanan for workshops in Body Mapping for conductors.